The History of the UK

CRAFTED BY SKRIUWER

Copyright © 2024 by Skriuwer.

All rights reserved. No part of this book may be used or reproduced in any form whatsoever without written permission except in the case of brief quotations in critical articles or reviews.

For more information, contact : **kontakt@skriuwer.com** (www.skriuwer.com)

TABLE OF CONTENTS

CHAPTER 1: THE EARLY SETTLERS AND PRE-ROMAN BRITAIN

- *Paleolithic and Mesolithic communities*
- *Neolithic Revolution and farming*
- *Megalithic monuments (e.g., Stonehenge)*
- *The Iron Age and tribal societies*

CHAPTER 2: ROMAN CONQUEST AND RULE

- *Claudian invasion of 43 CE*
- *Boudica's revolt and resistance*
- *Roman towns, roads, and baths*
- *Transition to post-Roman Britain*

CHAPTER 3: POST-ROMAN BRITAIN AND THE ANGLO-SAXON KINGDOMS

- *Collapse of Roman administration*
- *Anglo-Saxon migration and settlement*
- *Formation of early English kingdoms*
- *Christianity's resurgence*

CHAPTER 4: THE VIKING AGE AND THE DANELAW

- *Viking raids and settlements*
- *The Great Heathen Army*
- *Alfred the Great and Wessex's resistance*
- *Cultural blending in the Danelaw*

CHAPTER 5: THE NORMAN CONQUEST AND ITS IMPACT

- Battle of Hastings (1066)
- Feudal reorganization under William the Conqueror
- Domesday Book and centralization
- Harrying of the North and rebellions

CHAPTER 6: THE PLANTAGENETS AND THE GROWTH OF ROYAL POWER

- Henry II and legal reforms
- Thomas Becket and church-state conflict
- Early parliamentary developments
- Wars in France and territorial claims

CHAPTER 7: THE MEDIEVAL WARS AND SOCIAL CHANGES

- Edward II's downfall and baronial unrest
- Hundred Years' War beginnings
- The Black Death and its social impact
- Peasants' Revolt of 1381

CHAPTER 8: THE LATE MIDDLE AGES AND THE RISE OF THE TUDOR DYNASTY

- Wars of the Roses and dynastic battles
- Richard III, Bosworth Field (1485)
- Henry VII consolidates power
- End of medieval feudal structures

CHAPTER 9: THE TUDOR ERA – REFORMATION AND EXPLORATION

- Henry VIII's break with Rome
- Dissolution of monasteries
- Early overseas exploration (Cabot, Hawkins)
- Religious upheavals under Edward VI and Mary I

CHAPTER 10: THE ELIZABETHAN AGE AND CULTURAL FLOURISH

- Elizabeth I's religious settlement
- Defeat of the Spanish Armada (1588)
- Renaissance literature and drama (Shakespeare)
- Beginnings of England's maritime power

CHAPTER 11: THE STUARTS AND THE ENGLISH CIVIL WAR

- James I and divine right of kings
- Charles I's conflicts with Parliament
- Roundheads vs. Cavaliers
- Trial and execution of Charles I (1649)

CHAPTER 12: THE COMMONWEALTH AND THE RESTORATION

- Oliver Cromwell's Protectorate
- Religious and social experiments under Puritan rule
- Charles II's return (1660)
- Enduring impact of the Interregnum

CHAPTER 13: THE GLORIOUS REVOLUTION AND THE EARLY GEORGIAN ERA

- James II, Catholic tensions, and the 1688 revolution
- William III, Mary II, and the Bill of Rights
- Queen Anne and the Act of Union (1707)
- Rise of cabinet government (Walpole)

CHAPTER 14: GEORGIAN SOCIETY, INDUSTRY, AND COLONIAL AMBITIONS

- Hanoverian monarchs and political stability
- Agricultural improvements and early industrial changes
- Global trade, empire, and colonial wars
- American War of Independence and its effects

CHAPTER 15: THE ROAD TO THE UNION – SCOTLAND, IRELAND, AND WALES

- Highland Clearances and Scottish transformation
- Industrial stirrings in Wales
- 1798 Irish Rebellion and the Acts of Union (1800)
- Creation of the UK of Great Britain and Ireland (1801)

CHAPTER 16: THE NAPOLEONIC WARS AND THEIR EFFECTS ON BRITAIN

- Wars with Napoleonic France (1801–1815)
- Nelson's victory at Trafalgar, Wellington's campaigns
- Home front economy and social tensions
- Britain's emergence as a global naval power

CHAPTER 17: THE EARLY 19TH CENTURY – REFORM MOVEMENTS AND INDUSTRY

- Post-Napoleonic unrest (Corn Laws, Peterloo)
- Accelerating Industrial Revolution (railways, urban growth)
- 1832 Reform Act and Chartism
- Repeal of the Corn Laws (1846) and rise of free trade

CHAPTER 18: MID TO LATE 19TH CENTURY – VICTORIAN TRANSFORMATIONS

- Queen Victoria's reign and cultural accomplishments
- Further electoral reforms (1867, 1884)
- Social legislation (factory acts, public health)
- Imperial expansion and competition with rival powers

CHAPTER 19: THE DAWN OF THE 20TH CENTURY – IMPERIAL HEIGHT AND SOCIAL SHIFTS

- Edwardian era (1901–1910) and King Edward VII
- Liberal welfare reforms (pensions, National Insurance)
- Suffragette campaigns and Irish Home Rule crisis
- Naval arms race with Germany

CHAPTER 20: THE EARLY 1900S AND THE ROAD AHEAD

- World War I and its toll on Britain
- 1918 franchise expansion and rise of Labour
- Irish independence and partition (1921–1922)
- Transition to a more democratic yet challenged empire

Chapter 1: The Early Settlers and Pre-Roman Britain (circa 500,000 BCE–43 BCE)

Introduction

Pre-Roman Britain covers hundreds of thousands of years of human activity on the island. During this time, the land changed in climate, landscape, and resources. Groups of early humans wandered around, hunting and gathering, then later began farming and forming more permanent settlements. These changes did not happen suddenly, but they took shape slowly over long periods. By understanding each step, we see how Britain's early communities grew in complexity and laid the foundations for the societies that followed.

1.1 Britain's Ancient Landscape

During the earliest periods of human activity in Britain, the physical landscape was quite different. Over various ice ages, massive glaciers moved south and then retreated, altering the terrain and climate. At times, Britain was connected to continental Europe by land. This connection is often referred to as "Doggerland," which once joined Britain to what is now the Netherlands, Belgium, and parts of Germany. Early humans and animals could move freely across this land bridge. This meant that migrations were not as difficult as they later became after rising sea levels submerged these land connections.

The island's climate also shifted. During colder periods, ice sheets made the region nearly uninhabitable. In warmer periods, forests covered much of the land. Large herds of wild animals, such as deer and wild cattle, roamed these woods. Early groups of hunters followed them, setting up temporary camps. Over time, different species of humans, including Homo heidelbergensis and Neanderthals, passed through or settled in Britain for periods before either moving on or disappearing. Artifacts like flint tools have been discovered at sites such as Boxgrove in West Sussex, showing that people lived there roughly half a million years ago.

1.2 Paleolithic and Mesolithic Communities

During the Paleolithic era (Old Stone Age), people lived as nomads, relying on hunting and gathering for survival. These groups developed primitive stone tools, often made by striking flakes off flint nodules. The main goal was to create sharp edges for cutting meat or scraping hides. Hunting methods likely involved using simple wooden spears or driving animals into natural traps. Survival was hard, given the cold climate, wild predators, and limited technology.

Over time, the climate changed again. Some of these groups either died out or moved south, away from the colder northern regions. Then, as the climate warmed and the ice retreated, the Mesolithic era (Middle Stone Age) began. During this period, about 10,000 years ago, Britain became separate from mainland Europe when sea levels rose. The people who remained had to adapt to a more insular environment. They crafted microliths—small, sharp flint blades that could be set into wooden or bone handles to create more efficient tools. They also depended on fishing and smaller game, which were now more abundant in a warmer, forested environment.

Mesolithic communities still led mobile lives. They built temporary shelters, often near water sources like rivers, lakes, or coastal areas. Evidence of their campsites appears in the form of discarded flint pieces, fire pits, and animal bones. Life expectancy was short, and the population was small. But these groups learned to exploit a wide range of resources, including hazelnuts, berries, and fish. Slowly, people started to form seasonal patterns of movement, returning to certain sites year after year where they knew resources were plentiful.

1.3 The Neolithic Revolution in Britain

The shift from the Mesolithic to the Neolithic period (New Stone Age) marks a major turning point in Britain's history. This transition began around 4000 BCE, but it took hundreds of years for farming and settled life to spread throughout the island. The people who introduced these ideas likely came from the continent, bringing with them knowledge of plant cultivation and animal husbandry.

Instead of relying solely on wild resources, these new communities planted crops such as wheat and barley. They also domesticated animals like sheep, goats, cattle, and pigs. This allowed for a more predictable food supply, which in turn supported larger, more permanent settlements. Neolithic people no longer had to roam in small bands, though some communities still moved around a bit to find suitable grazing or farmland. Over time, more stable villages emerged.

With farming came changes in technology and culture. People began to polish stone tools for smoother, sharper edges. They also built long barrows, which were large burial mounds where groups of people were interred. These communal tombs reflect the development of more complex social structures. The dead were often buried with items like pottery or personal possessions, suggesting that people had new beliefs about the afterlife or the importance of community identity.

1.4 Megalithic Monuments and Social Complexity

One of the most striking features of Neolithic Britain is the construction of large stone monuments. These include henges, standing stones, and stone circles like Stonehenge and Avebury. Such monuments required tremendous effort, implying the existence of organized leadership or collective decision-making. Building something like Stonehenge, with its massive stones transported from miles away, shows that these communities were capable of significant planning.

Archaeologists have debated the purposes of these structures. They may have served religious or ceremonial functions, possibly relating to the changing seasons, ancestors, or the sun and moon. Whatever their exact use, they played a central role in the lives of Neolithic people. Over generations, these sites were modified and expanded, suggesting that they held long-standing importance.

This period also saw the emergence of pottery styles and the beginnings of more complex trade networks. Flint from specific regions, like Grimes Graves in Norfolk, was highly prized and traded. Axe heads made from unique stone outcrops traveled long distances, indicating that certain items had both practical and symbolic value. Communities likely interacted through seasonal gatherings, where goods, beliefs, and cultural practices were exchanged.

1.5 The Bronze Age and the Arrival of Metals

Between about 2500 BCE and 800 BCE, Britain underwent the transition from stone tools to bronze. This period introduced bronze as a new material for tools, weapons, and ornaments. The knowledge to smelt and cast metal probably arrived through maritime contact with mainland Europe. Bronze Age communities discovered how to mix copper and tin to create this durable metal, spurring changes in agriculture, warfare, and social ranking.

Bronze tools—such as axes, sickles, and spears—were more efficient than their stone counterparts. This encouraged surpluses in farming, which could then support larger populations. Also, social differences began to appear. The possession of metal goods could elevate a family's or individual's status. Those controlling the resources for bronze-making—like tin from Cornwall—could gain influence. Trade routes expanded, linking Britain with regions such as the Mediterranean, where metals and finished goods were exchanged.

Monuments changed in style. Round barrows became common, replacing long barrows of the Neolithic. These round burial mounds might hold a single wealthy individual or a small family group, often buried with metal objects, jewelry, or imported luxury items. This suggests that some people now held a higher place in society, one that allowed them more elaborate burial rites. Large hillforts also began to appear toward the end of the Bronze Age, though they became more widespread in the Iron Age.

1.6 The Iron Age and the Rise of Tribal Societies

Beginning around 800 BCE, iron started to replace bronze for tools and weapons. Iron ore was more plentiful in many parts of Britain, meaning local groups could produce it on a larger scale than bronze. Blacksmiths learned to smelt iron and hammer it into strong blades, ploughs, and tools. This had a major impact on farming, craftsmanship, and warfare.

Agricultural production improved as iron ploughs and sickles enabled people to work the land more efficiently. With more food, populations expanded, and new settlements appeared in various places, often near hilltops. Hillforts, which had begun in the Bronze Age, grew in size and number. They served as centers for trade, living, and protection. Some hillforts housed hundreds, even thousands, of people, hinting at organized communities under tribal leaders.

By this period, the island was divided into tribal areas, each led by a local ruler or chieftain. These tribal societies had their own customs, pottery styles, and trade links. Some minted their own coins, demonstrating that they had developed more advanced economies. The Iron Age saw the growth of warrior elites, who used iron swords and chariots in battle. Conflict between tribes was common, as they competed for farmland, cattle, and trade routes.

Religion and ritual continued to be important. Sacred groves, lakes, and rivers were often sites where valuables like swords or shields were deposited as offerings to gods. Druids, who were religious leaders in some Iron Age cultures, may have served as priests, teachers, and advisors, though details about them are still debated. The Romans, who later wrote about the Druids, viewed them with curiosity and sometimes fear, describing them as overseers of sacrificial rituals.

1.7 Influence of Continental Cultures

Although Britain sat off the European mainland, it was never fully isolated. Throughout the Iron Age, trade and cultural exchange with Gaul (modern-day France) and other regions of Europe was significant. Goods such as wine, olive oil, and metal wares arrived on British shores, while Britain exported metals, grain, and possibly slaves. Coastal tribes, especially in the southeast, had close ties to the continent, adopting certain styles of dress, art, and coinage.

By the first century BCE, Rome's reach began to affect Britain indirectly. Julius Caesar launched expeditions to Britain in 55 and 54 BCE. Although these invasions did not lead to permanent Roman occupation, they established some level of political influence. Many southern tribes recognized Rome's power, forging alliances or paying tributes. British leaders realized that a major shift in power loomed on the horizon.

In the years between Caesar's expeditions and the full Roman invasion under Emperor Claudius, British tribes continued to govern themselves. Some tribes built stronger fortifications, perhaps fearing renewed Roman aggression. Others sought advantages in trade or diplomatic relations with Rome. By the time Rome returned in 43 CE, Britain had multiple tribes of varying strengths, each with a distinctive culture but also subject to outside forces that would soon transform the island's future.

1.8 Transition to Roman Britain

When the Romans came in 43 CE, led by Aulus Plautius under orders from Emperor Claudius, Britain's Iron Age cultures were about to face major changes. Though this chapter ends at the brink of the Roman Conquest, it's important to note how the stage was set. The tribes were not unified under a single government, making it easier for Rome to ally with some while fighting others. Certain British leaders were already aware of Roman warfare tactics and political strategies because of earlier contact.

The rise of powerful tribal rulers, the growth of trade networks, and the continued building of hillforts all showed a dynamic, evolving society. While not as technologically advanced as the Romans, Iron Age Britons had strong warrior traditions, well-developed agricultural practices, and their own cultural richness. Their land was well worth conquering for Rome, which saw Britain as a source of valuable materials such as metals, grain, and possibly even manpower.

At the dawn of the Roman invasion, Britain was a collection of tribes, each with its own identity. The life of ordinary people varied from farmers to artisans to warriors. Despite never forming a single kingdom, these communities laid the groundwork for what would come. Their efforts in farming, building, and defending their land set an early template for how people interacted with Britain's varied landscapes. In the next chapter, we will see how Rome's arrival reshaped this world and left a lasting mark on British soil.

1.9 Summary of Chapter 1

From the earliest hunter-gatherers to Iron Age tribal groups, Britain's pre-Roman history covers a vast span of time. Each era introduced new ways of living, from nomadic hunts to settled farming. The land itself changed, sometimes connecting Britain to Europe and sometimes isolating it. Communities evolved from small camps to larger villages and hillforts, marking progress in social complexity, technology, and trade.

By the end of the Iron Age, Britain was no stranger to outside influence, engaging in trade with continental cultures and learning about Roman power. Yet, local identities remained strong. Tribes fought and cooperated among themselves in a patchwork of alliances. This environment set the stage for the dramatic shift that would come with Roman conquest. Understanding these first chapters of British history helps us appreciate how deep the island's cultural roots go and how many layers of human story lie beneath the surface.

Chapter 2: Roman Conquest and Rule (43 CE–410 CE)

Introduction

The Roman conquest of Britain began under Emperor Claudius in 43 CE, but it did not happen overnight. Rome had planned to take control for years, fueled by Julius Caesar's earlier expeditions. Once the legions arrived, they gradually expanded their reach across much of the island, establishing fortified towns and building roads. Roman occupation brought new technologies, art, trade, and ways of governance. However, it also brought rebellion and conflict. This chapter will outline how the Romans established their rule, what changes they introduced, and the nature of life in Roman Britain before Rome withdrew in the early 5th century CE.

2.1 The Claudian Invasion

In 43 CE, Emperor Claudius sent four legions, roughly 20,000 to 25,000 troops, to conquer Britain. This force was supplemented by auxiliaries—soldiers recruited from across the empire. The Roman general Aulus Plautius led the initial campaign, landing on the southeastern coast. One crucial step was to secure a beachhead and advance inland without facing overwhelming tribal resistance.

The Romans met resistance from tribes such as the Catuvellauni, led by Caratacus and his brother Togodumnus. The initial battles were fierce, but Roman discipline and superior military tactics gave them an edge. Togodumnus was killed, and Caratacus retreated westward, continuing to resist Roman advance. Emperor Claudius arrived later in person, partly for prestige, and to symbolically take control of the newly claimed territory. The city of Camulodunum (modern Colchester) became the first Roman capital in Britain, where Claudius accepted tribal submissions.

Following this early success, the Romans expanded their control. Legionary fortresses were established at key points, and roads were built to quickly move troops. Tribes that cooperated with the Romans could retain some level of autonomy under client-king arrangements, while tribes that resisted were often crushed, with their lands confiscated. Over time, more of the southeast came under Roman administration.

2.2 Caratacus and Resistance in Wales

One of the most notable tribal leaders to stand against Roman occupation was Caratacus (Caractacus), who moved west to rally support among the Silures and Ordovices in present-day Wales. He conducted a guerrilla-style campaign against Roman forces, using the mountainous terrain to his advantage. The Romans, led by generals such as Ostorius Scapula, found Wales challenging to conquer. The harsh landscape required fortresses and outposts to secure control.

Caratacus managed to evade capture for years, becoming a symbol of freedom for the tribes. However, after a significant defeat, he sought refuge among the Brigantes in northern England. Their queen, Cartimandua, had an alliance with Rome and handed Caratacus over to the Romans. He was taken to Rome as a captive, where, according to tradition, he impressed Emperor Claudius with his resolve. Instead of being executed, he was allowed to live in Rome, his defiance serving as both a trophy and a cautionary tale of Roman mercy and power.

Despite Caratacus's capture, revolt continued in Wales. The territory required a large military presence. Fortified towns like Deva (Chester) and Isca (Caerleon) served as strongholds for the legions. Eventually, through persistent campaigning, the Romans pacified these regions, but it was never a simple task, and tensions always simmered under the surface.

2.3 Boudica's Revolt (60–61 CE)

One of the most famous uprisings during the Roman period was led by Queen Boudica of the Iceni tribe. The Iceni, who lived in what is now East Anglia, had been a client kingdom of Rome. But when their king, Prasutagus, died, the Romans ignored his will, which left part of his estate to the emperor but also provided for his family. Roman administrators seized the kingdom, publicly flogged Boudica, and assaulted her daughters.

This treatment sparked a large-scale rebellion in 60–61 CE. Boudica rallied other tribes, including the Trinovantes, who resented Roman rule. They attacked and destroyed Camulodunum (Colchester), then marched on Londinium (London), which was evacuated by the Roman governor, Suetonius Paulinus. The rebels burned Londinium to the ground and then moved to Verulamium (St Albans), which they also destroyed. Archaeological evidence shows thick layers of burnt material from this revolt.

The turning point came when Suetonius Paulinus assembled his forces and confronted Boudica's army in a location most historians believe was somewhere in the Midlands. Despite being outnumbered, the Roman legions used superior tactics and discipline to crush the rebellion. Boudica's fate is uncertain—some sources say she took poison to avoid capture, others claim she died of illness. The uprising shook Roman confidence, but it ended in a Roman victory that tightened Rome's grip on Britain. Afterward, the empire implemented reforms to govern Britain more carefully, building new roads and fortifications while also trying to avoid unnecessary provocations.

2.4 Consolidation of Roman Rule

Following Boudica's revolt, Rome focused on consolidating its control. The province of Britannia was governed by a Roman-appointed governor, backed by a standing army of several legions and auxiliary units. The Romans built a network of roads including Watling Street, Fosse Way, and Ermine Street, facilitating trade and troop movements. Fortresses were established in strategic locations, and towns (coloniae) were formed for retired soldiers, such as at Camulodunum (Colchester), Lindum (Lincoln), and Glevum (Gloucester).

Urban centers like Londinium (London) grew rapidly into important trading and administrative hubs. Markets, baths, temples, and forums appeared, reflecting Roman city planning. Wealthy Britons and Roman settlers built villas in the countryside, some featuring mosaic floors, underfloor heating (hypocausts), and private bathhouses. Local elites who cooperated with Rome could become part of the Romanized aristocracy, gaining Roman citizenship and sometimes even positions in the empire's administration.

Still, not everyone prospered. Military service demanded local recruits. Heavy taxes paid for public works and the Roman army. Some native Britons may have felt sidelined or forced into lower-status roles. Yet, many also adopted Roman lifestyles. Over time, Latin became common in government and commerce, though native languages likely continued in private or rural settings. Temples built to Roman gods also sometimes incorporated local deities, merging traditions in a process called syncretism.

2.5 The Frontier: Hadrian's Wall and Beyond

As the Romans moved north, they encountered fierce resistance from tribes in what is now northern England and southern Scotland, including the Brigantes and the Selgovae. The emperor Hadrian visited Britain in 122 CE and decided to mark a clear northern boundary of the empire. This resulted in the construction of Hadrian's Wall, stretching across the narrowest part of northern Britain from the River Tyne to the Solway Firth. The wall, built primarily of stone and turf, featured forts, milecastles, and watchtowers, manned by auxiliary troops. It served as both a defensive line and a customs boundary for controlling trade and movement.

Later, Emperor Antoninus Pius briefly extended Roman control further north by building the Antonine Wall between the Firth of Forth and the Firth of Clyde. But maintaining this frontier proved difficult, and Rome eventually withdrew back to Hadrian's Wall. The northern tribes remained a continual challenge, leading to periodic campaigns under different governors. This frontier zone demonstrated Rome's intent to draw a line marking the extent of their empire. Within that boundary, they sought to create a stable province. Beyond it, local tribes continued to resist and raid.

2.6 Roman Society in Britain

Roman Britain became a blend of native and Roman customs. While the legions enforced peace, civilian life flourished in certain areas. Towns developed theaters, amphitheaters, and public bathhouses. Villas in the countryside produced grain, wool, and other goods for trade. The economy linked Britain to a vast network, reaching across the Channel to Gaul and beyond to the heart of the empire. Coins circulated widely, and markets thrived.

Local crafts benefited from Roman techniques in pottery, glassmaking, and metalwork. Samian ware (a type of fine pottery imported from Gaul) appeared in many settlements, while some local potteries began producing items in similar styles. Workshops near military forts produced weapons, armor, and everyday metal tools. Mosaic floors became a sign of wealth and status in villas, depicting geometric patterns or mythological scenes.

Religion was diverse. Official Roman gods like Jupiter, Mars, and Minerva had temples, but local deities continued to receive worship. The cult of Mithras, popular among Roman soldiers, built underground temples (mithraea). Over time, Christianity also arrived, probably in the 3rd century CE, and started gaining followers, though it was not dominant until centuries later. People in Roman Britain often merged beliefs, dedicating altars to hybrid deities that combined Roman and local traits.

2.7 Military Presence and Defense

Throughout the province, military forts and outposts provided security against external threats and internal rebellion. Apart from Hadrian's Wall, forts lined major roads and river crossings. Auxiliary units, recruited from across the empire—places like Germany, Spain, and North Africa—played a crucial role. These soldiers, once discharged, might settle in Britain, further adding to the province's cultural mix.

Inside these forts, life followed a strict schedule. Soldiers performed drills, maintained equipment, and patrolled nearby areas. They also built roads, bridges, and public buildings. The Roman army in Britain was a powerful institution that upheld Rome's authority, collected taxes, and enforced laws. The presence of the legions discouraged major uprisings, though smaller skirmishes with local tribes or raiders could still occur.

2.8 Economic Links and Changes

One of the major impacts of Roman rule was economic integration. Grain, cattle, wool, and minerals such as lead, tin, and silver were exported to other parts of the empire. In return, Britain received goods like wine, olive oil, and luxury items. Ports along the coast, like Londinium's harbor on the River Thames, facilitated trade. Roads connected these ports to inland towns, ensuring that supplies moved efficiently.

Roman coinage replaced or supplemented local currency. Taxation became more standardized, with assessments of land and property. This system could be heavy-handed, especially during periods of crisis when emperors demanded additional funds to support wars elsewhere. However, it also allowed for improved infrastructure—paved roads, aqueducts, and public buildings. For many Britons, this era brought increased stability in exchange for taxes and compliance with Roman law.

2.9 Revolt and the Limits of Control

Despite efforts to maintain order, Rome faced periodic unrest in Britain. For example, the governor Clodius Albinus attempted to declare himself emperor in 193 CE, marching his troops to Gaul to contest imperial authority. Although he was defeated, such events underlined how Britain could become a power base for ambitious generals.

Tribal unrest in the north and raids by groups such as the Picts (north of Hadrian's Wall) and the Scotti (from Ireland) tested Rome's frontier defenses. Sometimes, troops had to be pulled from Britain to deal with crises in other parts of the empire, weakening local stability. As the 3rd and 4th centuries progressed, the Roman Empire faced increased pressure from Germanic tribes on the continent. Emperors like Diocletian and Constantine the Great restructured the empire, dividing it into smaller administrative units. Britain became part of a larger diocese within the Western Roman Empire.

Still, cracks showed. Saxon raiders began to target Britain's east and south coasts. In response, Rome built a series of forts, known as the Saxon Shore forts, to repel these attacks. Yet the empire's ability to project power into Britain declined over time, leaving local authorities to handle increasing threats on their own.

2.10 The End of Roman Britain

By the early 5th century, Rome was under great strain. Barbarian groups were pressing into the Western Empire's borders. In 410 CE, the Visigoths sacked Rome itself—a catastrophic blow to imperial prestige. Around that time, Emperor Honorius is said to have told the civic leaders in Britain that they would need to look after their own defense. This is often cited as the formal end of Roman rule in Britain.

As the legions withdrew, Roman governance structures collapsed. Towns could no longer count on the empire for defense or funds. The villas and urban centers faced a decline, and roads were less maintained. Local leaders or warlords emerged to fill the power vacuum. Some Romanized Britons tried to maintain aspects of Roman life, but without the imperial system, many Romano-British customs withered.

Thus, Roman Britain dissolved into smaller, localized societies. Although the Roman Empire no longer ruled, its legacy endured. The roads, walls, villas, and towns left a mark on the landscape. Latin loanwords and certain administrative traditions would echo in the centuries to come. The stage was then set for new invaders—Anglo-Saxons and others—who would shape the next chapter of British history.

2.11 Summary of Chapter 2

Roman rule in Britain lasted roughly from 43 CE to 410 CE. During this period, the island underwent significant changes. The Roman military conquered and pacified various tribes, building roads and fortifications to secure their hold. Towns developed under Roman planning, and local elites were incorporated into the empire's governance. Trade expanded, reaching across a vast imperial network.

Yet, Roman domination was not uncontested. Famous revolts like those led by Caratacus and Boudica highlight the fierce resistance that occurred. Even after Rome established firmer control, the northern frontier remained a point of contention, resulting in the construction of Hadrian's Wall. Over time, the empire's internal struggles and external pressures weakened its grip. By the early 5th century, Rome withdrew from Britain, leaving behind infrastructure and cultural influences but no lasting central authority.

In the wake of this withdrawal, Britain entered a period of fragmentation and transition. Local leaders would soon face new challenges from migratory peoples. Nevertheless, Roman Britain forms a key chapter in the island's history, one marked by both conquest and cultural fusion. The next chapter explores the post-Roman era, when power shifts led to the formation of Anglo-Saxon kingdoms and shaped the identity of Britain for centuries to follow.

Chapter 3: Post-Roman Britain and the Anglo-Saxon Kingdoms (circa 410 CE–793 CE)

Introduction
After the Roman legions departed around 410 CE, Britain faced a time of uncertainty and change. The people who lived here could no longer rely on imperial forces for protection or guidance. Instead, local leaders, chieftains, and small warlords had to defend their lands against raids and new waves of migrants. Over time, several groups—most notably the Angles, Saxons, and Jutes—arrived from continental Europe. They established kingdoms that would grow into some of the earliest English-speaking polities. This chapter will explore how Roman influence lingered and changed, how new communities took shape, and how kingdoms emerged to set the stage for what would become England.

3.1 The Collapse of Roman Administration

When Roman authority withdrew from Britain, most of the formal structures of governance collapsed. Cities that had once flourished under Roman planning found themselves without the funds or organization to maintain public buildings, defenses, and roads. Town councils, once guided by Roman officials, struggled to collect taxes or enforce laws. As a result, some urban centers shrank drastically. In certain places, people abandoned large stone buildings in favor of smaller wood or wattle-and-daub houses.

Rural villas—country estates owned by Romanized British elites—were also affected. Without the central economic network that Rome had provided, many villa owners could no longer support their lifestyles. Trade slowed, especially the import of luxury goods like fine pottery or wine. Roads fell into disrepair, making it harder to move goods and people across long distances. The once-impressive aqueducts and bathhouses gradually decayed.

Still, some communities tried to keep Roman traditions alive. They adopted local leaders who might have had some experience with Roman administration, though these leaders lacked the manpower of the legions. In some regions, people continued to use Roman coinage or imitated Roman coin designs for a time, but there was no new official minting. Even though daily life was changing, the memory of Roman organization lingered in the cultural fabric.

3.2 Rise of Local Rulers and Early Kingdoms

With no central authority, power shifted to local strongmen who could defend a region. Some were former military commanders, others were tribal chieftains who had cooperated with Rome in the past. Over time, these local leaders carved out small territories. Fortified hilltops or the remains of Roman forts might become a base of operations. People needed security from raiders, so they turned to whomever could offer it, often trading labor or tribute for protection.

These warlords or kings formed the building blocks of the post-Roman political landscape. Although we do not have clear records of all these groups, archaeology suggests that many communities continued to farm and trade on a small scale. People still grew wheat and barley, herded livestock, and fished where possible. Crafts such as pottery and metalwork did not disappear but became more localized in style and distribution.

In some parts of western Britain, such as Wales and Cornwall, the native Brittonic-speaking population remained dominant. In the north, between Hadrian's Wall and the highlands of modern Scotland, various British and Pictish groups jostled for control. Over time, these regions developed their own traditions and legends, sometimes romanticized later as the time of King Arthur. Whether Arthur was a historical figure or not is still debated, but tales of a great war leader who defended the Britons against invaders reflect the struggles of this era.

3.3 Influx of Germanic Peoples: Angles, Saxons, and Jutes

Among the most significant changes of this period was the arrival of Germanic-speaking migrants from the European mainland. These groups included the Angles, Saxons, Jutes, and possibly Frisians. They came from areas around modern-day northern Germany and Denmark. The reasons for their migration remain a topic of debate, but likely included a mix of population pressure, opportunities for land, and invitations by some British rulers who needed help fighting rival groups or raiders from the north and west.

Initially, these Germanic warriors may have served as mercenaries, known as "foederati," under local British rulers. At some point, tensions arose, and the Saxon or Angle groups began to carve out their own territories in the eastern and southern parts of Britain. Over a few generations, more newcomers arrived, and settlements expanded. Archaeological evidence shows that these settlers brought their own burial customs, such as cremation urns and later furnished inhumation graves with weapons, jewelry, and daily items.

As these Germanic peoples established a foothold, British communities in the east were often displaced or absorbed. Some Britons fled west, into Wales or across the sea to Armorica (Brittany in modern France). Others stayed in their homelands but adapted to the new culture, eventually adopting the Anglo-Saxon language and ways. Over time, distinct Anglo-Saxon kingdoms began to form. Each had its own ruler, assemblies of warriors, and laws based on custom.

3.4 Formation of the Early Anglo-Saxon Kingdoms

By the 6th and 7th centuries, several Anglo-Saxon kingdoms emerged. Historians typically list seven major ones, calling them the Heptarchy: Northumbria, Mercia, East Anglia, Essex, Kent, Sussex, and Wessex. However, the situation was often more complicated, with sub-kingdoms and smaller polities existing at various times.

1. **Kent**: Traditionally associated with the Jutes, Kent was among the first areas where Germanic settlers gained permanent ground. The kingdom of Kent grew influential due to its proximity to continental Europe, facilitating trade and cultural exchange. Kent also became a major center for the introduction of Christianity when missionaries arrived from Rome.
2. **Sussex (South Saxons)**: Located along the southern coast, Sussex began as a smaller polity. Over time, its rulers sometimes allied with or fought against neighboring Wessex or Kent. The region's name reflects the Saxon heritage—"Suth Seaxe" meaning South Saxons.
3. **Essex (East Saxons)**: Northeast of London, Essex included areas on both sides of the Thames estuary. It had its own kings, some of whom converted to Christianity early on, though local pagan traditions often remained strong.
4. **East Anglia**: This region covered Norfolk and Suffolk, home to the Angles, and grew into a notable kingdom. East Anglia produced some of the most

famous archaeological finds, including the Sutton Hoo ship burial, which highlights the wealth and craftsmanship of early Anglo-Saxon elites.
5. **Northumbria**: Formed from two earlier kingdoms—Bernicia and Deira—Northumbria stretched from the Humber River north to modern-day Scotland. It became a powerful force in the 7th century, known for its cultural achievements, monastic sites, and scholarship.
6. **Mercia**: Located in the Midlands, Mercia grew to be one of the largest and most powerful Anglo-Saxon kingdoms under rulers like Penda (a pagan king) and later King Offa, who built Offa's Dyke along the border with Wales. Mercia's influence often rivaled that of Northumbria and Wessex.
7. **Wessex**: The West Saxons established themselves in the southwest. Over centuries, Wessex expanded, eventually becoming one of the most dominant English kingdoms. Later, it would play a leading role in unifying England in subsequent centuries.

These kingdoms did not emerge overnight. They took shape gradually, through alliances, warfare, and the assimilation of local populations. Borders shifted, and the balance of power changed often. Still, by around the late 7th century, a recognizable patchwork of Anglo-Saxon polities existed, setting the political stage for centuries to come.

3.5 Christianity and Missionaries

One of the most transformative developments of the early medieval period was the return of Christianity, though this time in a new form. While Roman Britain had some Christian communities, the departure of the legions and the arrival of pagan Saxons led to a decline in the visible presence of the Church in many areas. However, Christianity survived in places like Wales, Cornwall, and Ireland.

The reintroduction of Christianity to the Anglo-Saxons is traditionally traced to 597 CE, when Pope Gregory the Great sent Augustine (often called Augustine of Canterbury) to Kent. King Æthelberht of Kent allowed Augustine to preach and eventually converted to Christianity. This event triggered a broader missionary effort that spread throughout the Anglo-Saxon kingdoms, although conversion was a slow, uneven process.

Meanwhile, Irish missionaries played a significant role in converting and educating people in northern England and beyond. Monasteries like Iona (on the west coast of Scotland) and Lindisfarne (off the northeast coast of England) became centers of learning and spiritual life. Monks copied manuscripts, created elaborate artwork, and taught new clergy. Over time, the Roman and Celtic churches negotiated differences in customs, such as the dating of Easter, culminating in the Synod of Whitby in 664 CE, where King Oswiu of Northumbria chose to follow Roman practices.

As Anglo-Saxon rulers and elites adopted Christianity, they built churches and monasteries. They also sponsored the production of written texts in Latin, and, eventually, in Old English. This helped foster literacy among the educated class, though most common people remained illiterate. The spread of Christianity also influenced the legal system, leading to laws that reflected Christian morality, such as restrictions on certain types of violence or protection for the Church.

3.6 Art, Culture, and Society in Anglo-Saxon England

The Anglo-Saxon period saw the blending of Germanic traditions with residual Roman culture and emerging Christian influences. Material culture changed as Germanic styles in pottery, metalwork, and architecture merged with local and Mediterranean elements. Notable artifacts, like the treasures from Sutton Hoo, reveal a warrior culture that valued elaborate helmets, shield fittings, and gold and garnet jewelry. Art often featured animal interlace designs, stylized beasts, and geometric patterns.

Houses in Anglo-Saxon settlements were typically wooden structures with thatched roofs. Larger halls served as communal gathering places for feasts and assemblies. In time, stone churches and monasteries began to dot the landscape, reflecting the shift towards Christian practices. Society was stratified, with kings, ealdormen (noblemen), thegns (warrior retainers), and ceorls (freemen). At the bottom were slaves or bondservants. Loyalty between a lord and his warrior retinue was highly valued, forming the backbone of Anglo-Saxon military power.

Law codes in different kingdoms showed variations, but many shared core principles like compensation for injury (the wergild system). Crimes were often resolved by paying fines or through feuds, although the Church tried to encourage peaceful settlements. Women held various roles, sometimes inheriting property or managing estates in a husband's absence, though they were still under the legal authority of male relatives or husbands in most cases.

Anglo-Saxon literature flourished, including poetry composed in Old English. Works like "Beowulf" emerged from this oral tradition, eventually being written down in monastic scriptoria. Poems often celebrated heroism, loyalty, and the warrior ethos, while also weaving in Christian themes. Shorter elegies like "The Seafarer" and "The Wanderer" revealed a reflective, sometimes melancholic view of life, fate, and faith.

3.7 Political Shifts and Rivalries

Throughout the 7th and 8th centuries, power dynamics among the Anglo-Saxon kingdoms shifted frequently. At times, Northumbria was the most influential, as seen under King Edwin and King Oswald, both of whom played important roles in spreading Christianity. Northumbria's cultural output was remarkable, exemplified by the Lindisfarne Gospels and the scholarship of the monk Bede, who wrote the "Ecclesiastical History of the English People."

Mercia reached its peak under kings like Penda, who remained pagan for much of his rule and clashed with Christian neighbors, and later under King Offa (reigned 757–796 CE). Offa is famous for constructing Offa's Dyke, a large earthwork that roughly marked the boundary between Mercia and the Welsh kingdoms to the west. Mercia dominated much of southern England, at times subjugating other Anglo-Saxon rulers.

Wessex also rose to prominence near the end of the 8th century. Kings like Cædwalla and Ine expanded territory south and west, absorbing smaller groups. Wessex's fortunes would continue to grow into the 9th century, setting the stage for future kings like Alfred the Great, though that belongs to a later period. By the end of the 8th century, the Anglo-Saxon world had a patchwork of competing kingdoms, each with distinctive cultural traits, but also sharing common language, religion, and societal structures.

3.8 Influence of Ireland and the Picts

While Anglo-Saxon territories developed in what is now England, the lands to the north and west had their own trajectories. The Picts inhabited much of modern Scotland, while the Gaels in Dalriada (western Scotland) were connected to Ireland. Christian monasticism flourished in Ireland and was re-exported to

Britain through missionary work. Irish monastic schools became famous for their learning and artistry, producing illuminated manuscripts and spreading distinctive Celtic Christian practices.

In the region that would become Scotland, the kingdoms of the Picts and the Scots (Gaels) gradually merged. Over time, the expansion of the kingdom of the Scots reduced Pictish autonomy, though this process took centuries. Britain at this time was far from united; it was a mosaic of cultural zones, some Latinized from Roman days, others Germanic from the Anglo-Saxon influx, and yet others Celtic, preserving indigenous languages and traditions.

3.9 External Threats and Trade

Despite many local conflicts, the Anglo-Saxon kingdoms were not isolated. Trade routes connected them to the Franks on the continent, to the Irish Sea region, and even as far away as the Mediterranean. Goods like cloth, slaves, metals, and luxury items circulated. Missionaries and church scholars traveled widely, bringing manuscripts and theological ideas back and forth across the Channel. Diplomatic marriages and gift exchanges among royal families also fostered ties across the North Sea and beyond.

However, external threats existed. The coasts were vulnerable to seaborne raids, not only from rival British or Irish groups but also from new raiders who would soon appear in large numbers: the Vikings. By the late 8th century, occasional Viking attacks had begun, foreshadowing a more intense wave in the centuries to come. These early raids were often quick strikes on monasteries or coastal settlements, aimed at seizing wealth and slaves. The Anglo-Saxons were aware of this emerging threat but had not yet adapted their defenses to the extent required.

3.10 Transition to the Viking Age

In 793 CE, the famous Viking attack on the monastery at Lindisfarne shocked the Christian world. This event is often taken as the formal start of the Viking Age in Britain. Monastic chroniclers described the assault as a terrible calamity, though the Vikings had likely made smaller raids elsewhere before. Lindisfarne's destruction highlighted the vulnerability of rich monastic sites on Britain's coasts.

This moment marked a turning point. Over the next decades, more Viking ships would appear, attacking along river networks and establishing winter camps. The Anglo-Saxon kingdoms, already competing with each other, now faced a common external menace. Their political structures, defensive strategies, and even cultural identities would all be tested by these new pressures.

By focusing on the post-Roman era in this chapter, we have seen how Britain transformed from a province of the Roman Empire into a collection of independent kingdoms shaped by Anglo-Saxon culture. We explored how local leadership arose in the vacuum left by Rome, how Germanic groups settled and formed new societies, and how Christianity spread to become a unifying force. This sets the stage for the next major challenge to these kingdoms: the Viking invasions, which we will examine in the following chapter.

3.11 Summary of Chapter 3

Post-Roman Britain was a world in flux. The collapse of Roman structures left local rulers to fight for control, defend their people, and build new identities. Germanic peoples—Angles, Saxons, Jutes—established themselves in eastern and southern Britain, eventually forming various Anglo-Saxon kingdoms. Christianity, reintroduced by Roman and Celtic missionaries, played a key role in shaping culture, literacy, and law. Art, literature, and society combined elements of Germanic heritage, Roman tradition, and Christian belief to create something unique in early medieval England.

Although these kingdoms sometimes worked together, they often fought each other for dominance. Over time, powerful realms like Northumbria, Mercia, and Wessex emerged, each leaving its mark on the cultural landscape. To the north and west, Celtic peoples, Picts, and Gaels maintained their own distinct traditions, trading and at times clashing with the Anglo-Saxon realms. By the end of the 8th century, the stage was set for a new series of challenges—the Viking raids—that would reshape the political map of Britain once again.

Chapter 4: The Viking Age and the Danelaw (793 CE–1066 CE)

Introduction

The Viking Age in Britain began with a sudden and brutal attack on the monastery at Lindisfarne in 793 CE. Although smaller raids may have occurred prior to that year, Lindisfarne's fate signaled a wave of Norse expansion that would change Britain forever. In this chapter, we look at how Scandinavian raiders, settlers, and eventually armies arrived on the shores of Anglo-Saxon England, Ireland, and Scotland. They looted monasteries, seized lands for farming, and established new towns. Over time, a large swath of northern and eastern England became known as the Danelaw, reflecting Scandinavian legal and cultural influence. These developments forced the Anglo-Saxon kingdoms to adapt, unify, and fight back, shaping England's future in profound ways.

4.1 Early Viking Raids and Tactics

The Norse, commonly called Vikings, came from Norway, Denmark, and to some extent Sweden. They possessed advanced shipbuilding skills, crafting longships that could travel across open seas and navigate shallow rivers. This enabled them to strike quickly and retreat before local forces could mobilize. Early raids targeted monasteries and religious communities because they held valuable treasures, were often poorly defended, and stored wealth in the form of silver, gold artifacts, and books adorned with precious metals.

The attack on Lindisfarne was followed by raids on other coastal sites, such as Jarrow in Northumbria, Iona off the coast of Scotland, and various targets along the English and Irish coasts. Monastic chroniclers portrayed the Vikings as a scourge, describing their pagan rites and destructive behavior. While these accounts may be one-sided, there is no doubt the raids caused great distress and signaled a new era of warfare and plunder.

Over the next several decades, raids grew in frequency and scale. Sometimes the Vikings came in small groups seeking quick loot. At other times, larger fleets arrived, filled with warriors who wintered on British soil, building fortified camps and demanding tribute from local rulers. These seasonal invasions soon developed into more permanent settlements.

4.2 The Great Heathen Army and the Conquest of the North

A key turning point occurred in 865 CE when a large Viking army, often called the Great Heathen Army, landed in East Anglia. Led by brothers reputed to be sons of the legendary Viking Ragnar Lothbrok—among them Ivar the Boneless and Ubba—this force had far grander ambitions than simple raids. Their goal was to conquer and rule. They took horses in East Anglia and moved north, capturing the city of York in 866 CE. At the time, York was the capital of Northumbria, which was weakened by internal strife.

Northumbria fell quickly under Viking control. King Ælla, who was one of the local rulers, was killed in battle or captured. The Viking army then pushed south, targeting other Anglo-Saxon kingdoms. East Anglia itself was overrun, and King Edmund was famously martyred by the Norse. By 869, much of eastern England was in Viking hands. Mercia also suffered repeated invasions, and its king submitted to Viking overlords or lost territory.

This Viking force was well-organized, with enough manpower to occupy and defend seized lands. They established a stronghold at York (renamed Jórvík), which soon became a thriving Norse city. Archaeological digs in York reveal a rich mix of Anglo-Saxon and Scandinavian artifacts, suggesting a blending of cultures. Craftsmen worked in bone, wood, metal, and textiles, producing goods that reflected both Norse and local traditions.

4.3 Wessex Stands Firm: Alfred the Great

While Northumbria, East Anglia, and large parts of Mercia fell under Viking control, one kingdom resisted subjugation—Wessex. King Æthelred of Wessex fought against Viking incursions, but the pivotal figure of this era was his younger brother, Alfred, who later became known as "the Great." Alfred came to the throne in 871 CE when the Vikings were aggressively pressing into Wessex.

Alfred's early reign was marked by defeats and narrow escapes. In 878, the Vikings, led by Guthrum, launched a surprise attack during the winter, forcing

Alfred to retreat into the marshes of Somerset. There, he famously hid at Athelney and reorganized his forces. He rallied local militias (the fyrd) and launched a counterattack. In a decisive battle at Edington, Alfred's forces defeated Guthrum's army. As part of the peace settlement, Guthrum converted to Christianity, and Alfred stood as his godfather.

This victory did not end Viking threats, but it did establish a boundary between Alfred's kingdom and the territory under Danish control, known as the Danelaw. Over time, Alfred fortified Wessex by creating a network of burhs—fortified towns—that could provide quick defense against Viking raids. He also restructured the army, making sure only half were on duty at any time while the other half tended farms, ensuring a more stable resource base. Alfred's leadership allowed Wessex to survive as an independent kingdom. He also promoted learning, commissioned translations of Latin texts into Old English, and set the foundations for a more cohesive English identity.

4.4 The Danelaw: Scandinavian Settlements and Culture

The term "Danelaw" refers to the regions of England under Danish law and customs, roughly covering Northumbria, East Anglia, and parts of Mercia. Scandinavian settlers came not just as warriors, but also as farmers and traders. They integrated with local populations in many places, intermarrying and sharing cultural practices. Place names in the Danelaw often reflect Old Norse origins, with endings like "-by" (farm or village), "-thorpe," or "-toft." Many of these names endure in modern England, especially in Yorkshire and Lincolnshire.

The cultural exchange was significant. Norse language influenced Old English, contributing words related to law, seafaring, and everyday life. Archaeological evidence shows that some settlers retained pagan beliefs for a while, burying objects with the dead, though Christianization among the Vikings progressed over time. Churches in the Danelaw incorporated Scandinavian art styles, sometimes featuring runic inscriptions or stylized animals reminiscent of Norse carvings.

Economically, the Danelaw thrived on trade. York (Jórvík) became a major center, trading goods with the North Sea world and beyond. Coins minted under Viking kings used Christian symbols, hinting at the religious shift that was taking place. Despite their initial aggression, many Norse rulers recognized the benefits of commerce and stability. Over time, these territories produced hybrid cultures, neither fully Anglo-Saxon nor wholly Scandinavian, but a blend of both.

4.5 The Unification Efforts of the Wessex Kings

After Alfred the Great's reign, his successors continued to push against the Danelaw. His son, Edward the Elder (reigned 899–924), and daughter, Æthelflæd (the "Lady of the Mercians"), worked together to reclaim areas of eastern England. They built new burhs and took back strategic towns, gradually reducing Danish power. When Æthelflæd died, Mercia essentially came under the rule of Edward, further uniting the Anglo-Saxon response to the Vikings.

Edward's son, Æthelstan (reigned 924–939), extended control over Northumbria. In 937, Æthelstan's forces defeated a combined army of Vikings, Scots, and Strathclyde Britons at the Battle of Brunanburh, a major milestone in the push for unification. Æthelstan's triumph led later chroniclers to hail him as the first king of a united English nation, though actual administrative unity took more time to solidify.

Yet, Viking influence persisted. New waves of Scandinavian invaders came, including powerful leaders like Erik Bloodaxe, who briefly ruled York in the mid-10th century. The English kings had to maintain strong armies and alliances to keep control. The unification of England was a complex process, involving both warfare and political negotiation. Viking princes, at times, cooperated or competed with English rulers, depending on circumstances.

4.6 Renewed Viking Onslaught: The 10th and 11th Centuries

While the 10th century saw relative stability under kings like Edgar the Peaceful, the late 10th and early 11th centuries brought renewed Scandinavian pressure. Danish kings like Swein Forkbeard and his son Cnut launched massive invasions, partly triggered by English rulers paying large sums of money known as Danegeld to buy off raiders. These payments encouraged more Viking interest, as the riches of England became well-known.

In 1013, Swein Forkbeard successfully conquered most of England, driving King Æthelred the Unready into exile. However, Swein died soon after. His son, Cnut (also spelled Canute), returned to claim the throne. After a period of conflict, Cnut became King of England in 1016. He also ruled Denmark and Norway, forming a North Sea Empire that linked Scandinavia and Britain. Under Cnut's reign, England experienced a degree of prosperity and peace. He supported the Church, maintained a strong fleet, and integrated English and Danish nobles within his administration.

Yet this North Sea Empire did not last beyond Cnut's immediate heirs. When he died in 1035, his sons Harold Harefoot and Harthacnut struggled to hold the realm together. By 1042, the English throne reverted to the House of Wessex under Edward the Confessor. Even so, Scandinavian presence had deeply influenced English culture, law, and governance.

4.7 Social and Cultural Changes Under Viking Influence

The Viking Age brought many changes to everyday life. In areas under Norse control, local laws and customs often blended with those of the settlers. Old Norse words entered the English language, such as "law," "take," "window," "husband," and "skill." Trade towns grew, with improved craftsmanship in metalwork, woodworking, and textiles. Coinage systems sometimes displayed both Anglo-Saxon and Scandinavian symbols.

Art and architecture also reflected this fusion. Stone crosses in northern England displayed interlaced carvings that mixed Christian motifs with Norse serpents or dragons. Runic inscriptions sometimes appeared alongside Latin script. Nobles and merchants often traveled across the North Sea, creating a cultural interchange that went well beyond raiding. Monastic communities rebuilt after early raids, aided by patrons who were sometimes Viking converts to Christianity.

Women in Viking society, according to some sources, had relatively more freedom to manage property or maintain households during their husbands' absences. Some of these practices may have influenced local customs in the Danelaw. At the same time, the fundamental social hierarchy of lords, warriors, and peasants persisted, and slavery (including the taking of slaves during raids) remained a grim aspect of the era.

4.8 The End of the Viking Age in England

Although we often date the end of the Viking Age in England to the Norman Conquest of 1066, Scandinavian influence did not vanish overnight. Well before 1066, Vikings had integrated into English society, especially in the north and east. Many towns had substantial Scandinavian populations. Family names and place names in those regions still echo that heritage.

After Edward the Confessor's death in January 1066, several claimants vied for the English throne, including the Norwegian king Harald Hardrada. He invaded northern England and faced Harold Godwinson, the new English king, at the Battle of Stamford Bridge in September 1066. The English forces defeated and killed Harald Hardrada, marking a significant defeat of a major Viking leader. However, this victory was short-lived, as Harold Godwinson then rushed south to face another claimant—William, Duke of Normandy—who had invaded Sussex. William's victory at the Battle of Hastings in October 1066 changed English history in an entirely new direction.

Nevertheless, the Viking Age had already left its mark. The Danelaw's legal customs and the linguistic contributions of Old Norse shaped the development of Middle English. Many local traditions and place names remained part of the cultural landscape. Even the Normans themselves were descendants of Norse settlers in northern France, so in a roundabout way, the legacy of Viking expansion continued in the new rulers of England.

4.9 Scotland, Ireland, and the Isles

While this chapter mainly covers the Viking impact on England, it's important to note that Scotland and Ireland also experienced prolonged Norse influence. The Hebrides, Orkney, and Shetland Islands became heavily Norse in culture and governance. The Norse-Gael communities in the western isles were a blend of Gaelic and Scandinavian heritage. Powerful earls of Orkney emerged, who sometimes influenced mainland Scottish politics.

In Ireland, Vikings founded key coastal towns like Dublin, Waterford, and Limerick. They established trade networks that drew wealth into Ireland, though they also fought with local Irish kings. The Norse presence in Ireland persisted well into the 11th century, often merging with the local population over generations. Thus, the Viking Age was truly pan-British and pan-Irish, altering political, economic, and cultural trajectories across these islands.

4.10 Summary of Chapter 4

From the first recorded Viking raid at Lindisfarne in 793 CE to the Battle of Stamford Bridge in 1066, the Viking Age in Britain was marked by raids, conquests, settlements, and cultural blending. The most dramatic change came with the Danelaw, where Scandinavian rule reshaped large areas of northern and eastern England. Kings like Alfred the Great fought back, laying the foundations for a more unified English realm. Later, Cnut's brief North Sea Empire highlighted how intertwined Scandinavia and England had become.

Despite the violence of the initial incursions, the long-term legacy of the Vikings in Britain was not just destruction; it also encompassed settlement, trade, cultural exchange, and linguistic contributions that endure in modern English. By 1066, the English crown had faced—and sometimes embraced—Scandinavian rule and influence. Although the Norman Conquest ultimately ended Anglo-Saxon rule, it did not erase the Viking heritage already woven into the fabric of England.

This completes our examination of the Viking Age and the Danelaw. The next chapters will explore how the Norman Conquest brought a new elite to power and initiated another significant shift in culture, governance, and society in the British Isles.

Chapter 5: The Norman Conquest and Its Impact (1066 CE–1154 CE)

Introduction

In 1066, the landscape of England changed forever when Duke William of Normandy crossed the English Channel and defeated King Harold Godwinson at the Battle of Hastings. This event, known as the Norman Conquest, reshaped the country's rulers, culture, and social structures. Over time, new lords replaced much of the old Anglo-Saxon elite, and vast changes took place in landholding practices, architecture, and language. This chapter will look at the buildup to the Conquest, the key events in 1066, William the Conqueror's rule, and the ongoing transformations that affected the entire kingdom over the next century. We will also explore how the Normans extended their control across England and into parts of Wales, showing both the strengths and the tensions of this new regime.

5.1 Background and Claims to the Throne

After the death of King Edward the Confessor in early 1066, England lacked a clear plan of succession. Edward had no direct heir, which allowed various powerful figures to claim the throne. The strongest contenders were Harold Godwinson, a leading English nobleman and Earl of Wessex; Harald Hardrada, King of Norway; and Duke William of Normandy, who asserted that Edward had promised him the crown. Harold Godwinson managed to secure his coronation swiftly, but Duke William insisted he was the rightful successor based on agreements and oaths from previous years.

The Normans were descended from Viking settlers in northern France (the region of Normandy takes its name from the "Northmen"). Over generations, these Norse settlers had adopted French language and customs, becoming formidable feudal lords. William, sometimes called William the Bastard before he became "the Conqueror," was an ambitious and capable leader, determined to press his claim. Across the sea, Harold Godwinson readied his forces, while Harald Hardrada also eyed the English throne, creating a three-cornered rivalry.

5.2 The Battles of 1066: Gate Fulford, Stamford Bridge, and Hastings

Before William's invasion, England faced another crisis from the north. Harald Hardrada and Harold Godwinson's estranged brother, Tostig, launched a major invasion in Yorkshire. They defeated local English forces at the Battle of Gate Fulford on 20 September 1066. However, days later, King Harold Godwinson arrived with his army and surprised Hardrada's troops at the Battle of Stamford Bridge on 25 September. The English king won a decisive victory, killing both Harald Hardrada and Tostig. Although this success ended the Norwegian threat, it left Harold's forces fatigued and significantly reduced in number.

Meanwhile, William of Normandy landed on the south coast at Pevensey, setting up camp near Hastings. When King Harold heard the news, he rapidly marched south, hoping for a swift engagement to prevent William from entrenching. The two armies met at the Battle of Hastings on 14 October 1066. King Harold's forces formed a shield wall on Senlac Hill, while William's mounted knights and archers attempted to break through. The fighting lasted all day. In a critical moment, the Norman cavalry feigned retreat, drawing parts of the English line down the hill, where they were cut apart. Late in the day, King Harold was killed—legend says he was struck in the eye by an arrow, though the exact details are debated. With the death of Harold and much of his nobility, the English resistance collapsed. William emerged victorious.

5.3 William the Conqueror Takes Control

Following his triumph at Hastings, William moved methodically to secure the throne. He advanced toward London, encountering some local resistance, but key nobles realized they could not stop him. On Christmas Day 1066, William was crowned King of England at Westminster Abbey. However, conquering the throne symbolically was only part of the process. William needed to enforce his authority across a large, diverse kingdom that had just lost many of its leading men in battle.

William redistributed land to his Norman followers, granting them vast estates in exchange for military service and loyalty. This set up a new aristocracy. In many places, English earls and thegns (local nobles) were replaced by Norman lords, who built castles to control the countryside. Castles like Windsor, the White

Tower in London (later part of the Tower of London), and numerous motte-and-bailey structures popped up all over England. They served as defensive strongholds and a visual reminder of Norman power.

William also appointed Norman bishops and abbots to key positions in the Church, ensuring ecclesiastical backing for his regime. Archbishop Stigand, an Anglo-Saxon cleric, was replaced by Lanfranc, a reform-minded Norman. Although William cooperated with the Pope on some matters, he maintained that the English Church should stay under royal oversight. This balance between religious authorities and the Crown became a hallmark of Norman governance.

5.4 The Harrying of the North and Rebellions

In the years after Hastings, certain regions resisted Norman control, most notably the north of England. In 1069, a rebellion broke out involving Anglo-Saxon nobles, Danish forces who arrived to seek plunder, and local discontented peasants. William responded with ruthless efficiency. He marched north, destroying crops, livestock, and settlements in a campaign known as the "Harrying of the North." Thousands of people died from famine, and large swathes of Yorkshire were left desolate for years. While this brutal action suppressed resistance, it also caused long-term damage to an entire region and remains a stark example of medieval harshness in warfare.

Smaller revolts occurred in the West Midlands and in East Anglia, where an English rebel named Hereward the Wake famously led resistance from the marshes of Ely. These pockets of revolt were eventually crushed, or the rebels were forced to flee. By the early 1070s, William had broken the back of major opposition, though resentment lingered among the native populace. The new Norman aristocracy consolidated landholdings, imposing feudal obligations and introducing Norman customs in areas that had been largely Anglo-Saxon.

5.5 Domesday Book and Centralized Rule

To strengthen royal administration and secure revenue, William commissioned a massive survey of his kingdom in 1085–1086, resulting in the Domesday Book. This document recorded who held each piece of land, how it was used, and what resources it produced. It was intended to ensure that taxes and feudal duties were properly assessed and collected, giving William a powerful tool to manage the economy and keep his nobles in check.

The Domesday Book reveals many aspects of 11th-century England: population distribution, agricultural practices, and how land was consolidated under the Normans. The scope of this survey was unprecedented in medieval Europe. People called it "Domesday" because they felt it was final, like the Day of Judgment—there was no appeal against its findings. With this detailed information, William created a centralized administration that, in many ways, extended the efficiency of earlier Anglo-Saxon tax systems while layering on new feudal obligations.

5.6 Norman Governance and Feudalism

Under William, a feudal system became more structured, though historians debate how much of it was genuinely new versus older Anglo-Saxon traditions that the Normans adapted. In simplified terms, William was the supreme landlord, and his greatest supporters (barons, earls, and bishops) held lands known as fiefs, granted by the king in return for military service. These barons, in turn, could have knights who held smaller parcels of land. At each level, loyalty and obligations flowed upward, with protection and land tenure flowing downward.

The feudal structure also influenced justice and administration. Sheriffs, who had existed under the Anglo-Saxon kings, continued in their roles but were often replaced by Normans. They represented the king in the shires, collecting taxes, enforcing law, and calling out the local militia (the fyrd) when needed. As Norman French became the language of the ruling elite, English remained the common tongue of peasants, though it started absorbing French vocabulary. Over time, this blend would help shape Middle English.

5.7 Norman Culture and Architecture

The Normans introduced distinctive Romanesque architecture. This style is marked by rounded arches, thick walls, and massive proportions. Many cathedrals and abbeys were rebuilt in this new fashion, replacing older Anglo-Saxon churches. Examples include Durham Cathedral (begun in 1093), which showcases early advanced Romanesque or proto-Gothic features, and parts of Winchester Cathedral. Castles, primarily of the motte-and-bailey type, appeared across the countryside. They featured a wooden (later stone) keep on a raised earth mound (motte) and a walled courtyard (bailey).

Culturally, Norman nobles brought a different style of warfare, emphasizing heavy cavalry. Tournaments and chivalric ideals gradually took shape, though formal chivalry as we recognize it developed more fully in later centuries. The arts saw new influences in illuminated manuscripts and ecclesiastical design. The mix of Norman and Anglo-Saxon traditions produced a rich tapestry of customs over time, reflected in everything from local laws to the foods served at noble banquets.

5.8 William's Later Reign and Succession Struggles

William spent much of his reign traveling back and forth between England and Normandy, securing both realms against threats. He faced ongoing conflicts on the continent, battling neighboring French lords and dealing with rebellious sons. His final years were marked by tension within his own family over who would inherit what. In 1087, William was injured during a campaign in northern France and died soon after. He divided his holdings between his sons: Robert got Normandy, and William Rufus (William II) received England. This division created lasting friction, as each son envied the other's territory and power.

William II (often called William Rufus, from his red hair) ruled England from 1087 until 1100. He was energetic, forceful, and seen by some churchmen as irreverent toward religion. He continued to face rebellions led by Norman nobles who felt closer to Robert or desired more autonomy. He also undertook wars in Normandy to expand his control. William Rufus died in 1100 under mysterious circumstances—a hunting accident in the New Forest, though some suspect foul play. His younger brother, Henry, seized the royal treasury and had himself crowned King Henry I of England before Robert could act.

5.9 Henry I and the Centralization of Royal Power

Henry I (1100–1135) proved to be a shrewd and capable king. He quelled opposition early on and took steps to strengthen royal governance. He issued the Charter of Liberties, promising to respect certain church rights and feudal obligations, which some see as a precursor to later documents like the Magna Carta. Henry married Edith (renamed Matilda), a daughter of the Scottish royal house and descendant of the Anglo-Saxon kings. This helped heal some rifts between Norman rulers and their English subjects, while linking Henry to ancient English royalty.

Henry also focused on administrative reforms. He streamlined the royal household, introduced more systematic financial accounting (the Exchequer), and continued the use of writs to convey royal commands across the kingdom. The Exchequer's "Pipe Rolls" became a key mechanism for tracking revenues, fines, and debts owed to the Crown. Henry spent much of his reign trying to control Normandy, clashing with his brother Robert. Eventually, he captured Robert and held him prisoner for the rest of Robert's life, uniting England and Normandy under one ruler once again.

However, tragedy struck in 1120 with the sinking of the White Ship, in which Henry's heir, William Adelin, drowned. This left Henry with no legitimate son to succeed him. He named his daughter, the Empress Matilda (widow of Holy Roman Emperor Henry V), as his heir. But many nobles remained uneasy about the idea of a female monarch, setting the stage for a future succession crisis.

5.10 The Anarchy under Stephen

When King Henry I died in 1135, his nephew Stephen of Blois quickly raced to England and had himself crowned King Stephen. He claimed he acted to prevent unrest, but in truth he was taking advantage of the uncertain succession. Empress Matilda contested Stephen's right to the throne. The result was a lengthy civil war (1135–1153), often called "The Anarchy." Many barons switched sides depending on political advantage, and lawlessness spread across the country as central authority weakened.

Matilda's strongest support came from her half-brother, Robert of Gloucester, and her uncle, David I of Scotland. King Stephen faced constant challenges to his authority, and at times he was even captured by Matilda's forces. However, Matilda herself found little popularity among the Londoners, who forced her to flee the city. The conflict dragged on for years with no decisive winner. Some areas of England suffered widespread devastation as local lords exploited the power vacuum.

Eventually, a compromise was reached: Stephen would rule for the rest of his life, but he recognized Matilda's son, Henry of Anjou, as his successor. This arrangement ended the civil war in 1153. When Stephen died in 1154, Henry of Anjou ascended the throne as King Henry II, founding the Plantagenet dynasty and ushering in a new chapter of English history.

5.11 Norman Influence on Wales and Scotland

During the Norman period, efforts to expand control over Wales and Scotland also took shape. Norman lords built castles in the border regions known as the Welsh Marches. Some Norman knights carved out semi-independent lordships, pushing into parts of southern Wales. In northern areas, Welsh princes resisted, and the rugged landscape made permanent conquest difficult. Still, the Normans established footholds that would shape Anglo-Welsh relations for centuries.

Scotland maintained relative independence under kings like Malcolm III and David I. David I, who had spent time at the Anglo-Norman court, introduced Norman feudal practices to Scottish governance. He encouraged Norman nobles and monks to settle, founding abbeys and building castles. The result was a partial "Normanization" of Scotland, though it retained its own royal lineage and laws. The blend of Celtic traditions with Anglo-Norman influences set the stage for future interactions between England and Scotland.

5.12 Lasting Changes from the Norman Conquest

By the mid-12th century, the Norman Conquest had transformed England in ways that would endure for centuries:

1. **Feudal Structures**: Landholding patterns were reorganized under a strict hierarchy, creating a new aristocracy that owed direct allegiance to the king.
2. **Castles and Fortifications**: The Norman emphasis on building motte-and-bailey and later stone castles permanently changed the physical landscape, with many surviving fortifications still visible today.
3. **Language and Culture**: Norman French became the language of the royal court and nobility, influencing vocabulary, law, and literary traditions. Over time, this merged with Old English, leading to Middle English.

4. **Legal and Administrative Systems**: William and his successors refined tax collection, justice, and administration, partly by blending Norman feudal ideas with older English institutions. The Domesday Book stands as a monument to this systematic approach.
5. **Ecclesiastical Reforms**: The Normans reformed and reorganized the English Church, adding continental ties and building grand Romanesque cathedrals.
6. **Dynastic Tensions**: Divisions between Normandy and England became a recurring theme, leading to frequent conflicts and shaping the monarchy's focus on both sides of the Channel.

5.13 The Broader Significance of Norman Rule

The Norman Conquest brought a new ruling elite who reshaped England's identity. Nobles of Anglo-Saxon descent either lost power or married into Norman families, merging traditions. Even though the Conquest was violent and disruptive, it also spurred cultural exchange. Over time, the differences between Norman and English customs began to blur, forming a distinct English identity that included French linguistic and cultural elements.

The Norman kings also kept close ties with the continent, affecting alliances, rivalries, and military campaigns for generations. England was no longer isolated on the edge of Europe; instead, it was deeply linked to Normandy and other parts of France. This entangled relationship would eventually lead to major events like the Angevin Empire under Henry II and the long series of conflicts known later as the Hundred Years' War.

5.14 Summary of Chapter 5

The Norman Conquest of 1066 was a turning point, uprooting the Anglo-Saxon political order and installing William the Conqueror as king. Norman rule introduced new aristocrats, feudal customs, and architectural styles. The Domesday Book demonstrated a remarkable capacity for centralized governance, while the Harrying of the North showed the often brutal methods of control.

Succession crises, like The Anarchy under Stephen, highlighted the fragility of Norman leadership when clear heirs were absent. Nonetheless, by the mid-12th century, a blended Anglo-Norman realm had taken root, with Henry II poised to launch the Plantagenet era. The conquest's effects resonated far beyond the immediate generation, influencing legal, cultural, and social developments that shaped the medieval kingdom.

The next chapter will focus on the Plantagenet dynasty, which took power in 1154 and oversaw another significant phase of expansion, legal reform, and internal tensions that set the course of English history for centuries.

Chapter 6: The Plantagenets and the Growth of Royal Power (1154 CE–1307 CE)

Introduction

When Henry II ascended the throne in 1154, he founded what is now commonly called the Plantagenet dynasty. These kings oversaw major changes in law, governance, and territorial expansion, shaping the kingdom's identity further. Henry II's marriage to Eleanor of Aquitaine and his claims in France created a vast dominion known as the Angevin Empire. Under his rule and those of his sons, England strengthened the royal courts, established important legal precedents, and wrestled with the Church for power. Great conflicts and agreements emerged, including the murder of Thomas Becket and the drafting of the Magna Carta. This chapter will cover the period from Henry II's accession to the early 14th century reign of Edward I, examining how the Plantagenets tightened their grip on power, dealt with rebellions, and set the stage for later medieval England.

6.1 Henry II: The Early Years and the Angevin Empire

Henry II (1154–1189) was the son of the Empress Matilda and Geoffrey, Count of Anjou (whose badge was a sprig of broom plant, or "planta genista," from which "Plantagenet" originates). By his mother's lineage, Henry inherited a claim to the English throne. Through his father, he gained the county of Anjou. He also married Eleanor of Aquitaine in 1152, acquiring one of the largest and wealthiest domains in France. When he became King of England, Henry ruled over territories stretching from the Scottish border down through Normandy, Anjou, Aquitaine, and even parts of Ireland later.

Henry was energetic, determined, and focused on restoring strong royal authority after the chaos of Stephen's reign. Early on, he reclaimed royal castles from barons who had built them without permission during The Anarchy. He traveled frequently across his lands, asserting his presence and making sure local officials remained loyal. Although he delegated power to regional administrators, he never let them operate entirely free of supervision.

6.2 Legal Reforms and the Royal Court System

A hallmark of Henry II's reign was his legal and administrative reforms. He strengthened the royal courts, making "king's justice" more accessible. The Assize of Clarendon (1166) and subsequent Assizes introduced the concept of juries of presentment—groups of local men who would report crimes in their area. This laid the groundwork for what became the grand jury system. In addition, royal justices traveled on circuit (the "eyre") to hear cases, reducing the power of local feudal lords who once held near-complete authority in their own territories.

Henry II also popularized the use of "writs"—royal orders with standardized forms—that provided clear legal instructions. The practice of appealing directly to the king's court became more common, bypassing local baronial or manorial courts. Over time, this growth in royal justice eroded feudal fragmentation and centralized legal authority under the Crown. Common law started to take shape, based on precedent and consistent procedures, setting England apart from many continental systems that relied more on Roman law codes.

By increasing royal involvement in justice, Henry boosted the monarchy's prestige and revenue, as court fees and fines flowed into the royal treasury. These reforms made him popular with many ordinary freemen who saw royal courts as potentially more impartial than local lords. However, powerful barons resented the erosion of their traditional privileges.

6.3 Tensions with the Church: Thomas Becket

One of the most famous conflicts of Henry II's reign involved Thomas Becket, the Archbishop of Canterbury. Originally, Becket had been the king's chancellor and close friend, known for his administrative efficiency. When the archbishop's seat became vacant in 1162, Henry appointed Becket, expecting him to support royal interests in church affairs. However, once installed as Archbishop, Becket shifted his loyalty to the Church, vigorously opposing any encroachment by the Crown on ecclesiastical privileges.

The key issue was the extent to which churchmen could be tried in royal courts rather than in ecclesiastical courts. Henry argued that "criminous clerks" who committed serious offenses should not escape harsh penalties. Becket insisted that the Church had its own judicial system, and the king had no right to override it. Their dispute escalated, leading to Becket's exile. Efforts to reconcile failed as both sides refused major compromises.

In 1170, four knights, interpreting the king's heated words as a command, traveled to Canterbury and murdered Becket in his own cathedral. Shockwaves spread throughout Christendom. Henry II performed public penance and had to accept certain concessions, though he continued to preserve much of his legal control. Becket's martyrdom ultimately strengthened the Church's moral authority in the eyes of many, even though Henry retained practical power.

6.4 Conflict within the Royal Family: Rebellions of Henry's Sons

Henry II's later years were troubled by rebellions led by his own sons, encouraged at times by Queen Eleanor. The king's sons—Henry the Young King, Richard (later the Lionheart), Geoffrey, and John—chafed under their father's tight control. They wanted their inheritances to be handed over sooner, or at least to have more autonomy. In 1173, the three eldest sons rose in revolt, supported by Eleanor and aided by the French king and some Anglo-Norman barons unhappy with Henry's authority.

Henry II managed to crush these rebellions, though not without difficulty. He showed a degree of mercy to his sons, but the family tensions never fully disappeared. Eleanor was placed under house arrest for a time. Eventually, Henry's eldest surviving son, Richard, rebelled again with the support of the French king, Philip II. Henry II, physically weakened by illness and betrayed by his favorite son, John, died in 1189. Richard succeeded him as King Richard I, known as Richard the Lionheart.

6.5 Richard the Lionheart and the Crusades

Richard I (1189–1199) spent very little time in England. He saw the kingdom primarily as a source of revenues to fund his military campaigns, especially the Third Crusade (1189–1192). Richard was renowned for his bravery and skill in battle. He fought against the Muslim leader Saladin in the Holy Land, achieving some victories but failing to retake Jerusalem permanently. While returning from the Crusade, he was captured and imprisoned by Duke Leopold of Austria, prompting England to pay a heavy ransom for his release.

During Richard's absences, governance fell largely to officials like William Longchamp or to his younger brother, Prince John, who tried to secure power for himself. Richard eventually returned to England briefly, received new funding, and then focused on wars in Normandy against the French king. In 1199, he died from a crossbow wound while besieging a castle in France. With no legitimate heirs, the crown passed to his brother John, marking a pivotal shift in English royal fortunes.

6.6 King John and the Loss of French Territories

John (1199–1216) inherited the Angevin Empire, but he faced immediate challenges. French king Philip II took advantage of John's perceived weakness to seize large parts of Normandy, Anjou, and Touraine. By 1204, John had lost most of his ancestral lands in northern France, earning him the nickname "John Lackland." This loss diminished the English crown's continental power and forced John to rely more heavily on resources from England and remaining territories like Gascony and Poitou in southwestern France.

John's relationship with his nobles and the Church deteriorated. He quarreled with Pope Innocent III over the appointment of the Archbishop of Canterbury, leading to England's excommunication and an interdict that closed churches and withheld sacraments. John eventually submitted to the Pope, even becoming a papal vassal to secure an alliance against France. Meanwhile, his demands for high taxes to fund failed attempts to regain French lands angered the barons.

6.7 The Road to Magna Carta

Baronial discontent peaked in 1214 when John's campaign in France ended in the disastrous defeat at the Battle of Bouvines. Returning home with little to show for his expensive war effort, John faced open rebellion. A group of barons demanded reforms, standing up against what they saw as John's arbitrary and unfair rule. By 1215, they captured London and forced John to negotiate. At Runnymede, they drafted a charter that limited the king's ability to levy taxes and abuse feudal privileges.

This document, known as the Magna Carta (Great Charter), was sealed by King John on 15 June 1215. It asserted that the king was not above the law, guaranteeing rights like protection from illegal imprisonment and swift justice. It also stated that certain taxes required the "common counsel" of the realm, an early step toward parliamentary principles. Although John soon appealed to the Pope to annul the charter, Magna Carta set a critical precedent. Future kings would face re-issues and expansions of its clauses, embedding the idea of a contract between ruler and ruled in English political life.

6.8 The First Barons' War and Transition to Henry III

Almost immediately after sealing Magna Carta, John reneged on its terms. This triggered the First Barons' War (1215–1217). Some rebellious barons invited Prince Louis of France to claim the English throne, and he landed in England. John's death in 1216 from dysentery abruptly changed the situation. His nine-year-old son became King Henry III, and key royal officials, led by the great knight William Marshal (Earl of Pembroke), acted as regents.

William Marshal reissued Magna Carta in Henry's name, calming many barons who preferred a native English king to a French prince. Over time, the French forces withdrew. Henry III's early reign involved repeated struggles with influential barons, but also an ongoing effort to strengthen and expand the monarchy's legitimacy. The young king grew up believing in the special holiness of kingship and poured resources into building projects like Westminster Abbey.

6.9 Henry III: Challenges and Parliament's Beginnings

Henry III (1216–1272) reigned for 56 years, a period marked by ongoing tensions between the Crown and the barons. He made expensive attempts to regain lost French territories and favored certain foreign advisers from Poitou and Savoy, stirring resentment among English nobles. In 1258, a group of barons forced Henry to agree to the Provisions of Oxford, which established a council of 15 to advise the king and laid out regular parliaments—an unprecedented step toward representative government.

One major figure in this period was Simon de Montfort, Earl of Leicester. At first, he was a trusted ally and brother-in-law to the king, but later led a rebellion. De Montfort's forces captured Henry and his son, Prince Edward (the future Edward I), at the Battle of Lewes in 1264, effectively controlling the government. During his rule, De Montfort called a famous parliament in 1265 that included knights and burgesses from towns—often considered a milestone in the development of the English Parliament. Eventually, Prince Edward escaped, rallied royalist supporters, and defeated De Montfort at the Battle of Evesham (1265). Despite De Montfort's defeat, the precedent for broader parliamentary involvement had been set.

6.10 Edward I and the Conquest of Wales

Henry III's son, Edward I (1272–1307), is remembered for his military campaigns, administrative reforms, and efforts to strengthen royal authority. After returning from crusading in the Holy Land, Edward inherited the throne. Early in his reign, he took steps to confirm and enforce earlier charters but also to assert the Crown's prerogatives. He systematically reformed the law courts, earning the nickname "the English Justinian" from some chroniclers.

A key part of Edward's reign was his conquest of Wales. The Welsh prince Llywelyn ap Gruffudd had expanded his power, claiming recognition as Prince of Wales. Edward, seeing this as a challenge, led major campaigns from 1277 to 1283. He built imposing stone castles such as Caernarfon, Conwy, and Harlech to secure these territories, using advanced military architecture. By the end of these campaigns, Wales was effectively under English control, and Edward named his eldest son "Prince of Wales," a tradition that continues for heirs to the English (and later British) throne.

6.11 Wars with Scotland and the Emergence of Scottish Resistance

Edward I also turned his attention north, intervening in the Scottish succession crisis after the death of King Alexander III. In 1292, he chose John Balliol as king but demanded fealty as overlord of Scotland. Balliol resisted, leading to conflicts known as the Wars of Scottish Independence. Edward's forces invaded, deposed Balliol, and seized the Stone of Destiny from Scone Abbey, symbolically affirming English overlordship.

Resistance soon rose under figures like William Wallace, who defeated an English army at the Battle of Stirling Bridge in 1297. Edward responded harshly, defeating Wallace at Falkirk in 1298. Wallace was captured and executed in 1305. Another rebel, Robert the Bruce, emerged as a leader of the Scots. Though Edward I died in 1307 while campaigning north, the struggle continued under his son, Edward II. The Wars of Scottish Independence shaped Scottish identity and challenged England's desire to dominate the entire island.

6.12 The Growth of Parliament and Taxation

Under Edward I, the role of parliament expanded. The king frequently summoned knights, burgesses, and nobles to gain consent for taxes. Known as the "Model Parliament" of 1295, it included representatives from shires and towns, reinforcing the principle that taxation required some form of common consent. This development was partly due to Edward's constant need for funds to wage wars in Wales, Scotland, and on the continent.

This broader participation did not mean a modern democracy, but it did signal that the monarchy recognized the need to negotiate with various social strata, especially as the cost of warfare escalated. Over time, these assemblies evolved into two houses: the House of Lords (high nobility and clergy) and the House of Commons (knights and burgesses). These changes laid the groundwork for future constitutional developments.

6.13 Social and Economic Life Under the Early Plantagenets

During the Plantagenet period, England's economy and society experienced growth and complexity. Agriculture was the mainstay, but towns expanded, becoming centers for crafts, trade, and guilds. London, in particular, thrived as a commercial hub, with merchants trading wool and other goods. The Church remained a dominant force, running schools, hospitals, and monasteries. Universities like Oxford and Cambridge began to take shape, slowly evolving into leading centers of learning.

Feudal obligations were still strong, but the rise of a money economy allowed many peasants to pay rents instead of labor services. This process, sometimes called commutation, eroded the strict manorial system, though large swathes of the population remained unfree serfs (villeins). Fairs and markets became central to local economies, and trade relationships with continental Europe expanded. Medieval guilds governed trades and crafts, setting standards and prices.

The Plantagenet kings also encouraged the settlement of foreign merchants and craftsmen, hoping to stimulate economic development. Jewish communities, invited by the Norman and early Plantagenet rulers, played an important role in moneylending and finance, although they faced periodic persecution and heavy taxation. Over time, tensions led to the expulsion of Jews in 1290 by Edward I, reflecting the era's prejudices.

6.14 The Legacy of Henry II to Edward I

From Henry II's ascension in 1154 to Edward I's death in 1307, England underwent significant changes:

1. **Legal Evolution**: Common law began to form as royal courts and circuit justices became more robust. Key legal documents like Magna Carta put constraints on the Crown and recognized baronial and common rights.
2. **Territorial Ambitions**: The kingdom's reach extended into Wales through conquest, while repeated wars sought control of Scotland. The dream of continental dominance waned after major losses in Normandy, yet English kings continued to assert claims in France.
3. **Parliamentary Foundations**: Frequent parliaments under Henry III and Edward I introduced a broader representation of knights and townspeople in taxation decisions, planting seeds for modern parliamentary institutions.
4. **Royal and Ecclesiastical Struggles**: Tensions between kings and popes, as well as disputes over church appointments, shaped political and religious landscapes. The murder of Thomas Becket became a symbol of ecclesiastical defiance against royal interference.
5. **Economic and Social Growth**: Population increases and urban development fueled economic expansion. The feudal system adapted as monetary rents replaced some labor services, while trade and guilds flourished in growing towns.

6.15 Summary of Chapter 6

The Plantagenet era, starting with Henry II, continued the process of centralizing royal authority begun under the Normans. Henry II's legal reforms, combined with his determination to control both Church and baronial power, greatly expanded the Crown's influence. The dramatic conflict with Thomas Becket showed the limits of that power when faced with moral and spiritual authority.

Despite internal family rebellions, Henry's empire spanned large portions of France and the British Isles. However, under King John, the monarchy suffered humiliating losses in Normandy and faced baronial rebellion at home, resulting in Magna Carta—a foundational document for constitutional governance. Henry III struggled to maintain balance with his barons, and new forms of parliamentary representation emerged. Edward I, through conquests and administrative skill, solidified the monarchy's standing but also set the stage for further conflict, particularly with Scotland.

By 1307, England was a more centralized realm than it had been under the early Norman kings, with established institutions for law, taxation, and limited representation. The next chapters will explore how these foundations held up through the later Middle Ages, including the crises of the Hundred Years' War, the Black Death, and the internal strife that eventually reshaped the English monarchy again.

Chapter 7: The Medieval Wars and Social Changes (1307–1381)

Introduction

By 1307, England was under the rule of Edward I's son, Edward II. The kingdom's governance had become more centralized thanks to reforms in law and parliament, but strong monarchs were still crucial to maintaining stability. This chapter will examine how Edward II's weak leadership led to turmoil and how his son, Edward III, started the famous Hundred Years' War against France. We will look at the impacts of major battles, the catastrophic Black Death, and the deep social changes these events caused. We will end with the Peasants' Revolt of 1381, a direct sign of the shifting power dynamics in medieval English society.

7.1 The Accession of Edward II

When Edward I died in 1307, his son Edward II inherited the throne. Edward I had been a powerful, reform-minded king, known as the "Hammer of the Scots" for his campaigns north of the border. In contrast, Edward II lacked his father's military skill and political acumen. He also had favorites at court, granting them positions of influence that angered many nobles.

The most notorious of these favorites was Piers Gaveston, a Gascon knight. Edward II lavished titles and honors upon him, even naming him the Earl of Cornwall. English barons resented Gaveston's sudden rise, seeing it as an insult to the old nobility. Tensions worsened as Edward ignored his council's advice in favor of Gaveston's counsel. Some historians suggest a deep personal attachment between Edward and Gaveston, though the exact nature of their relationship remains debated. Regardless, the king's favoritism soon stirred open hostility among influential peers who felt sidelined.

7.2 Growing Baronial Discontent

England's barons had grown accustomed to a certain balance between royal authority and their own privileges, especially under Edward I, who skillfully used parliament to manage the realm. Under Edward II, the political environment deteriorated. Gaveston's arrogance and lavish lifestyle offended older, more established noble families. In 1311, a group of powerful barons, often referred to as the "Ordainers," drafted a series of ordinances to limit the king's ability to make appointments and handle finances without their approval. They demanded Gaveston's exile, arguing that his presence disrupted the kingdom's governance.

Edward II was forced to comply for a time, but he soon defied the barons by recalling Gaveston. Conflict erupted, leading to Gaveston's capture by baronial forces in 1312. They executed him, claiming they were acting in the kingdom's best interest. Edward II swore vengeance, but he lacked the military and political strength to punish those responsible fully. The barons had shown they could directly challenge the king, setting a precedent for further unrest.

7.3 Scotland's Rise: The Battle of Bannockburn (1314)

While England's internal disputes raged, Scotland continued to assert independence. Robert the Bruce, having crowned himself King of Scots in 1306, took advantage of England's political weakness. Edward II tried to restore English dominance over Scotland but was neither as strategically capable nor as determined as his father. In 1314, he led a sizable English army north to relieve the besieged Stirling Castle, hoping to reassert control.

The opposing forces met at the Battle of Bannockburn. The Scottish army was smaller, but Bruce's positioning and tactics exploited the terrain and forced the English cavalry into cramped, marshy ground. The English knights, accustomed to open-field charges, struggled to maneuver. Scottish spearmen inflicted heavy losses, and Edward II's army broke in a panic. Bannockburn was a major Scottish victory, boosting Robert the Bruce's legitimacy and weakening England's grip on Scotland. It remains one of the most celebrated battles in Scottish history.

7.4 The Rise of the Despensers and Edward II's Downfall

After Bannockburn, Edward II's prestige hit a low point. England's nobles increasingly blamed the king's poor leadership for the disaster. A new set of royal favorites emerged, chiefly Hugh Despenser the Younger and his father, Hugh Despenser the Elder. They gained power and vast estates, antagonizing other barons just as Gaveston had done. By 1321, a group of Marcher Lords (powerful nobles on the Welsh border) revolted, hoping to remove the Despensers. Edward crushed the rebellion, exiling some barons and executing others.

The king's harsh reprisals fueled more resentment, even within the royal family. Edward's wife, Queen Isabella—daughter of the French king—grew alienated from her husband due to the Despensers' influence. In 1325, Isabella traveled to France, ostensibly to negotiate peace with her brother, King Charles IV. While there, she formed an alliance with Roger Mortimer, one of the exiled Marcher Lords, and began plotting Edward II's overthrow.

In 1326, Isabella and Mortimer invaded England with a small force. Many nobles and common people joined them, furious at Edward II's misrule. The king fled but was captured in Wales. Parliament then forced Edward to abdicate in favor of his teenage son, who became Edward III. Edward II was imprisoned, and in 1327 he died in suspicious circumstances, likely murdered on the orders of Mortimer and the new regime. Isabella and Mortimer ruled as regents for the young Edward III, dominating the government much as the king's favorites once had.

7.5 Edward III and the Beginnings of a New Era

Edward III (1327–1377) grew up watching the chaos of his father's reign and the controlling influence of Mortimer and Isabella. In 1330, at age 17, Edward III acted decisively. He staged a coup, arresting Mortimer and taking full royal authority into his own hands. Mortimer was executed for treason, and Isabella was retired from power. The young king then sought to restore prestige to the Crown.

One important aspect of Edward III's strategy was to revive the concept of chivalry and knightly virtue, hoping to unite his nobles under a shared martial culture. He founded the Order of the Garter in 1348, dedicated to Saint George, as a symbol of knightly fellowship. Alongside this, he supported the growth of parliament, realizing that cooperation with the nobility in matters of taxation and warfare could strengthen his position. Edward also took a keen interest in warfare and dreamed of reclaiming territories on the continent once held by his ancestors.

7.6 The Hundred Years' War: Causes and Early Conflicts

The Hundred Years' War is generally dated from 1337 to 1453, though it involved periods of truce. Its root cause lay in conflicting claims over the French throne and control of territories in southwestern France. When the last Capetian king died without a direct male heir, Edward III—who was related to the French royal line through his mother—claimed the French crown. The French nobility rejected his claim in favor of Philip VI of the Valois family. Edward III's attempt to press his right triggered a struggle that would last, intermittently, for over a century.

Initially, the war was mostly fought on French soil. Edward III launched raids, known as chevauchées, to weaken the French economy. The English naval victory at the Battle of Sluys (1340) secured control of the Channel for some time, allowing easier transport of troops and supplies. Edward also built alliances with Flemish cities, who resented French interference in the wool trade. This complex web of treaties, marriages, and pledges shaped the early phases of the conflict.

7.7 The Battles of Crécy and Poitiers

Two major battles marked England's initial successes. The first was the Battle of Crécy (1346), where Edward III's army, though outnumbered, defeated Philip VI's forces. English longbowmen played a decisive role, unleashing rapid volleys of arrows that disrupted French cavalry charges. The English also used defensive positions effectively, with dismounted knights and men-at-arms forming strong lines. The French knights, steeped in traditional chivalry, launched repeated frontal attacks that ended in disaster.

A decade later, at the Battle of Poitiers (1356), Edward III's son, the Black Prince (Edward of Woodstock), achieved another stunning victory. Again, the longbow proved lethal against French charges. The French king, John II, was captured, an event that embarrassed the French court and forced them to negotiate. The subsequent Treaty of Brétigny (1360) granted England large territories in France in exchange for King John's release. However, the English gains were never fully secure, and warfare flared up repeatedly.

7.8 The Black Death (1348–1350)

Amid these military triumphs, England—and much of Europe—faced an even greater crisis: the Black Death. This pandemic, commonly attributed to bubonic plague, arrived in England in 1348, likely through merchant ships docking at southern ports. It spread rapidly, killing a significant portion of the population in just a few years. Estimates vary, but between one-third and one-half of England's people may have perished in the initial outbreak.

Villages were left deserted, fields went untilled, and labor shortages became widespread. Fear and superstition abounded. Many believed the plague was divine punishment for human sin. Religious processions, self-flagellation movements, and scapegoating of minority groups occurred across Europe. In England, traditional funeral practices faltered because there were too many corpses for normal burials. Mass graves, or plague pits, were dug in many urban areas, including London.

7.9 Social and Economic Transformations

The Black Death accelerated social changes already underway. With fewer peasants available to work the land, surviving laborers found they could demand higher wages. Many landowners tried to enforce old feudal obligations, preventing peasants from leaving or asking for better terms. In response, the government issued measures like the Ordinance of Labourers (1349) and the Statute of Labourers (1351), designed to freeze wages at pre-plague levels and restrict workers' mobility. These laws were largely ineffective, as laborers, in practice, could seek more favorable conditions and simply move if they were not satisfied.

Feudalism began to weaken as a direct result of the labor shortage. Manor lords, faced with unworked lands, increasingly commuted labor services to cash rents. This shift gave peasants a chance to buy or lease land more freely, improving their status slightly. In towns, craftsmen and merchants often found more opportunities, as the reduced population created a demand for specialized goods and services. Over time, a new middle stratum emerged, bridging the gap between traditional nobility and the peasantry.

7.10 Parliament's Growing Role

Amid the social upheaval, parliament gained a larger voice in governance. Edward III needed funds for his campaigns in France, so he regularly summoned parliaments to approve taxation. Knights of the shire and burgesses from towns attended alongside lords and bishops. Over the decades, these "Commons" formed a separate body that discussed and negotiated taxation with the king's ministers. In return for granting taxes, they began to present petitions on matters of law and policy, slowly expanding their influence.

By the mid-14th century, the House of Commons was taking shape as a distinct chamber. While still far from modern democratic principles, this development laid groundwork for future constitutional evolution. The Commons could withhold or reduce grants of money if the king did not address their grievances. Royal power, though still vast, increasingly depended on winning the cooperation of leading men from across the realm.

7.11 Edward III's Later Reign and the Good Parliament (1376)

As Edward III aged, his once-vibrant leadership waned. His eldest son, the Black Prince, was a brilliant commander but suffered from poor health. By the 1370s, the king faced mounting debts, declining military fortunes in France, and a royal court rife with corruption. Edward III's younger son, John of Gaunt (Duke of Lancaster), emerged as a key figure, but he was unpopular with many people who blamed him for mismanagement and high taxes.

In 1376, the so-called "Good Parliament" met. Led by the Commons, members demanded reforms and the removal of corrupt officials close to the Crown. They were partially successful; several of Edward's advisers were dismissed or impeached. However, after the parliament dissolved, John of Gaunt reversed many of its actions. The event still showed that parliament could flex its muscle, reflecting widespread frustration with the administration.

7.12 The Accession of Richard II

Edward III died in 1377, leaving his grandson Richard II as king. Richard was just ten years old. The Black Prince had died the previous year, so the line of succession passed to Richard. During his minority, a council of nobles governed, but powerful figures like John of Gaunt retained major influence. The realm continued to struggle with the costs of ongoing war in France and the fallout from the plague.

Richard II's coronation offered hope for a renewed monarchy, but he inherited daunting challenges. The war effort in France had stagnated, taxes were high, and social unrest festered. The poll taxes introduced to finance campaigns abroad fueled growing anger among commoners. Many peasants and artisans felt they should not bear the brunt of funding the nobility's overseas ambitions, especially since their own living conditions remained precarious after the plague.

7.13 The Peasants' Revolt (1381)

The tension finally erupted in 1381 with the Peasants' Revolt, one of the most famous uprisings in English history. Sparked by attempts to collect a new poll tax, crowds of peasants and townspeople from Kent and Essex marched on London. Their leaders included figures like Wat Tyler and the preacher John Ball, who challenged the traditional social order. Ball famously declared, "When Adam delved and Eve span, who was then the gentleman?"—a clear statement against the idea of inherited nobility.

Rebels attacked symbols of authority, damaging property owned by unpopular officials, and even storming the Tower of London, where they seized and beheaded the Archbishop of Canterbury, Simon Sudbury, who was also the Chancellor. King Richard II, still a teenager, agreed to meet the rebels at Mile End and Smithfield. He promised reforms, such as ending serfdom and pardoning those involved in the uprising. However, in a confrontation at Smithfield, Wat Tyler was killed, and the momentum of the revolt dissipated. Once the rebels dispersed, royal forces suppressed remaining pockets of resistance. The king's promises were quickly revoked.

While the revolt was brutally put down, it left a strong impression. The social contract was shifting: peasants had openly challenged their lords, demanding recognition of their rights and an end to feudal constraints. Although serfdom did not end overnight, the revolt hastened its decline. Over the coming decades, more peasants secured their freedom or moved to wage-based arrangements. The monarchy learned to be more cautious in imposing direct, nationwide poll taxes. Parliament, representing many landowners who had faced attacks, also recognized the need for compromise between different social classes to maintain stability.

7.14 Summary of Chapter 7

From the troubled reign of Edward II to the crisis of the Peasants' Revolt under Richard II, this era was one of upheaval and transformation. Edward II's weakness led to baronial domination and set England on a path of internal conflict, culminating in his forced abdication. Edward III brought military glory in France and fostered a blossoming parliament, but the Black Death wreaked havoc across the social and economic landscape. Labor shortages empowered common people to negotiate better terms, while the monarchy's need for funding gave parliament more leverage. By the late 14th century, the old feudal order was weakening, and the seeds of a more flexible social structure were taking root.

In the Peasants' Revolt of 1381, ordinary workers demanded equality and an end to oppressive taxes. Although the uprising itself was crushed, it revealed a new awareness among the lower orders that they had bargaining power. Over the next century, England would continue to face challenges at home and abroad. Our next chapter will cover the later Middle Ages, focusing on the final stages of the Hundred Years' War, the internal conflicts known as the Wars of the Roses, and the eventual victory of the Tudor dynasty in 1485—a moment that set the stage for early modern England.

Chapter 8: The Late Middle Ages and the Rise of the Tudor Dynasty (1381–1485)

Introduction
By the early 1380s, England had weathered both the Black Death and the Peasants' Revolt. King Richard II, still a teenager, seemed poised to either repair royal authority or sink into new crises. Meanwhile, the Hundred Years' War with France continued in the background, draining finances and morale. Over the next century, England saw major swings of fortune in France, a growing sense of national identity, and severe internal power struggles culminating in the Wars of the Roses. This chapter will explore Richard II's turbulent reign, the emergence of the Lancastrian kings, the victories and defeats in France under Henry V and Henry VI, and the dynastic battles that ended with Henry Tudor's triumph at the Battle of Bosworth in 1485.

8.1 The Early Reign of Richard II

After the Peasants' Revolt, the young Richard II appeared to side with the nobility, retracting most concessions given to the rebels. His reign continued under the shadow of influential figures like John of Gaunt, but as Richard matured, he sought to govern more independently. He cultivated the idea of a majestic kingship, emphasizing ceremony and chivalric ideals. He also favored a circle of close advisers, alienating some older nobles who saw themselves as natural counselors to the king.

Conflict arose in the 1380s between Richard's court and a group of high-ranking nobles known as the Lords Appellant. They accused some of the king's favorites of mismanagement and treason, leading to the "Merciless Parliament" of 1388, which condemned several of the king's associates. Richard was forced to submit, but he never forgot this humiliation. In the 1390s, he gradually rebuilt royal authority and took revenge on those who had challenged him.

8.2 Richard II's Downfall

By the late 1390s, Richard II had become more autocratic. He imposed harsh penalties on those who opposed him and manipulated legal procedures to target his enemies. Such tactics bred fear and resentment. His cousin, Henry Bolingbroke (John of Gaunt's son), fell victim to the king's spite, being exiled and disinherited. When John of Gaunt died in 1399, Richard seized Gaunt's lands instead of letting Henry inherit them.

Seizing the opportunity, Henry Bolingbroke returned from exile while Richard II was on a campaign in Ireland. Many English nobles, angry at the king, rallied to Henry. Faced with little support, Richard was captured and forced to abdicate. Henry proclaimed himself King Henry IV. Richard was imprisoned, and he died in captivity under suspicious conditions—likely murdered or starved in early 1400.

Henry IV's usurpation established the Lancastrian line of the Plantagenet family on the throne, shifting power from one branch to another. This event also raised profound questions about the nature of kingship and the right to rule. Going forward, the monarchy's legitimacy would face further scrutiny, especially during periods of weakness or internal strife.

8.3 Henry IV and Domestic Turmoil

Henry IV (1399–1413) began his reign with fragile legitimacy, having deposed an anointed king. Various rebellions and conspiracies arose, including plots by Richard II's remaining supporters and challenges from Wales, where Owain Glyndŵr led a major revolt for Welsh independence starting in 1400. Henry spent much of his rule quelling uprisings. His reliance on parliament to raise funds further strengthened the Commons' role in governance, continuing a trend from earlier decades.

Glyndŵr's revolt raged in Wales for several years, gaining initial successes and capturing key castles. However, Henry's forces, aided by internal divisions among the Welsh, eventually contained the rebellion. By the early 1410s, Glyndŵr had lost much of his support. Nonetheless, the Welsh uprising showed that local populations could challenge English rule effectively if the crown's hold was weak.

8.4 The Glory of Henry V

Henry IV died in 1413, passing the throne to his son, Henry V (1413–1422). Energetic and ambitious, Henry V is best known for renewing the war in France with stunning success. Early in his reign, he cracked down on domestic dissent, including an attempted Lollard uprising led by Sir John Oldcastle. After securing peace at home, Henry turned his attention to France, seeing an opportunity to claim lands he believed were rightfully English.

In 1415, Henry V invaded Normandy. Despite facing overwhelming odds, he achieved a legendary victory at the Battle of Agincourt (25 October 1415). The English army, weary and outnumbered, used the longbow to devastating effect. French knights, bogged down in muddy fields, fell in large numbers. Agincourt became a symbol of English prowess and bolstered Henry's reputation as a chivalric hero. Over the next few years, he conquered large parts of northern France, culminating in the Treaty of Troyes (1420), which recognized Henry as heir to the French throne and regent of France during the life of King Charles VI. Henry sealed this arrangement by marrying Charles VI's daughter, Catherine of Valois.

8.5 Henry VI and the Loss of French Territories

Henry V died unexpectedly in 1422, leaving an infant son, Henry VI, as King of England and nominally of France. A regency council governed in Henry VI's name. At first, English fortunes in France remained stable, with key strongholds in Normandy and beyond. However, the rise of Joan of Arc in 1429 reignited French resistance. Joan's victories at Orléans and other battles helped crown Charles VII as the rightful French king at Reims. English forces gradually lost ground, suffering from insufficient reinforcements and divisions among their commanders.

Back in England, Henry VI came of age, but he lacked the leadership qualities of his father. Deeply pious and prone to periods of mental breakdown, Henry struggled to manage court factions and the ongoing war. As French armies recaptured territory, it became clear that the English hold on France was slipping. By 1453, after losing the key region of Gascony, England retained only Calais on the continent. The dream of a dual monarchy in England and France effectively ended.

8.6 Seeds of the Wars of the Roses

While English military fortunes declined overseas, political tensions mounted at home. Two major noble factions coalesced around different branches of the royal family: the Lancastrians (supporters of King Henry VI) and the Yorkists, led by Richard, Duke of York, who had his own claim to the throne through his Plantagenet lineage. Henry VI's bouts of insanity and the strong influence of his wife, Margaret of Anjou, alienated many nobles. Some viewed the duke of York as a more capable leader who could stabilize the realm.

From 1450 onward, sporadic conflicts flared between supporters of the crown and York's allies. The first major clash was at the First Battle of St Albans in 1455, where Richard of York emerged victorious over Lancastrian forces. Although the conflict quieted temporarily, deep grievances remained. The battles that followed over the next three decades would become collectively known as the Wars of the Roses, named after the badges associated with each faction: the red rose for Lancaster and the white rose for York.

8.7 The Wars of the Roses: Key Phases

The Wars of the Roses were not one continuous war but rather a series of campaigns, battles, and uneasy truces. Several main phases emerged:

1. **1455–1461**: After St Albans, the Yorkist faction seized control of the government, with Richard of York becoming Protector during Henry VI's incapacities. However, Margaret of Anjou raised Lancastrian armies, culminating in a series of engagements. Notably, the Battle of Wakefield (1460) saw Richard of York killed. His son, Edward, carried on the Yorkist claim.
2. **Edward IV's Ascendancy (1461–1470)**: In 1461, Edward, Richard of York's son, won a decisive victory at the Battle of Towton, one of the bloodiest battles on English soil. Henry VI fled, and Edward was crowned King Edward IV. The Lancastrians continued to resist, but Edward consolidated power. For a time, relative peace prevailed as he established a Yorkist court.
3. **Lancastrian Revival and Warwick's Rebellion (1470–1471)**: Edward IV fell out with his major supporter, Richard Neville, Earl of Warwick—known as the "Kingmaker." Warwick briefly restored Henry VI to the throne in 1470. But Edward returned from exile, defeated Warwick at the Battle of Barnet

(1471), and crushed the remaining Lancastrians at the Battle of Tewkesbury. Henry VI was captured and died soon after, effectively ending major Lancastrian resistance.
4. **Richard III and the Princes in the Tower (1483–1485)**: After Edward IV's death in 1483, his young son, Edward V, was set to inherit. However, Edward's brother, Richard, Duke of Gloucester, claimed the throne as Richard III, alleging the young prince was illegitimate. The boy king and his brother, famously known as the Princes in the Tower, disappeared, and rumors spread that they had been murdered. This move alienated many Yorkists, who sided with Henry Tudor, a Lancastrian claimant by distant lineage.

8.8 The Rise of Henry Tudor

Henry Tudor (also known as Henry VII) spent years in exile in Brittany, waiting for a chance to press his claim. He had a tenuous but legitimate Lancastrian connection through his mother, Margaret Beaufort, descended from John of Gaunt. With Richard III deeply unpopular after the disappearance of the Princes in the Tower, Henry sensed an opportunity. In August 1485, Henry Tudor landed in Wales with a small army, receiving support from Welsh nobles and various disaffected English lords.

The decisive confrontation came at the Battle of Bosworth Field (22 August 1485). Richard III fought bravely but lost crucial support when some of his allies defected to Henry during the battle. Richard was killed on the field, and Henry Tudor emerged victorious. He was crowned King Henry VII, marking the official start of the Tudor dynasty. This event ended the main phase of the Wars of the Roses, although minor threats and pretenders would appear later.

8.9 Social and Economic Change in the Late Middle Ages

Even as the nobility battled for the throne, wider social and economic shifts continued:

- **Rise of the Gentry**: Many lesser landowners, or gentry, gained influence by managing estates efficiently and by supporting or opposing various

factions at court. Their local power and wealth sometimes surpassed that of older noble families devastated by the wars.
- **Growth of Towns**: Trade and commerce expanded in cities like London, Bristol, and York. Merchant and craft guilds controlled local economies, setting standards for prices and quality. Some merchants grew extremely wealthy, financing shipping ventures and building grand houses.
- **Agricultural Adjustments**: The old feudal obligations continued to loosen. Landowners, needing revenue, rented out land on more flexible terms. Peasant farmers sometimes pooled resources to rent or buy land collectively. While outright serfdom still existed in pockets, the momentum was towards wage labor and tenancy arrangements.
- **Cultural Developments**: Literacy spread slowly, aided by the growth of grammar schools and the early influence of the printing press (introduced to England by William Caxton in 1476). Religious literature and pious texts circulated more widely. Lay piety movements, some influenced by Lollard ideas (followers of John Wycliffe), questioned aspects of Church wealth and organization, although outright heresy was still harshly punished.

8.10 Language, Literature, and Identity

During the late medieval period, the English language gained status. Following the Norman Conquest, French had been the language of court and administration, while Latin dominated the Church and legal documents. By the 15th century, English reemerged as the main language of royal proclamations and literature. Writers such as Geoffrey Chaucer (1343–1400) produced notable works in Middle English, including "The Canterbury Tales," reflecting a diverse range of social voices.

The Hundred Years' War, ironically, fostered a stronger sense of English identity by pitting the kingdom against France for generations. Nobles who once spoke French at home came to see themselves as English aristocrats fighting for an English cause. The conflict over the French crown lost momentum, but it left behind cultural unity that would carry into the Tudor era.

8.11 Conclusion of the Wars of the Roses

Although Bosworth (1485) is often considered the war's end, a final skirmish happened at Stoke Field in 1487, where Henry VII defeated the forces of a Yorkist pretender, Lambert Simnel. Another pretender, Perkin Warbeck, emerged in the 1490s, claiming to be one of the missing Princes in the Tower, but he too was eventually captured and executed. Henry VII, through careful diplomacy, strategic marriages, and financial management, gradually brought stability to a realm weary of noble strife.

The monarchy under Henry VII also enhanced its fiscal base by enforcing royal dues and avoiding expensive foreign wars. This approach, combined with dynastic marriages—like his son Arthur's marriage to Catherine of Aragon—opened a new phase in relations with other European powers. While all this belongs partly to the early Tudor story, the seeds were planted in the last decades of the 15th century.

8.12 The Dawn of the Tudor Age

By 1485, after a century of intermittent warfare in France and decades of internal conflict, England stood on the threshold of a new era. The medieval period, defined by feudal structures and chivalric warfare, was transitioning into the early modern period, marked by stronger centralized monarchies, new forms of diplomacy, and evolving economic practices. Henry VII's reign symbolized recovery and renewal.

Under the Tudors, the English Crown would assert a power not seen since the days of the strongest Plantagenet kings, but with a different character—less reliant on baronial support and more focused on bureaucratic governance. Parliament would remain significant, though the monarchy sought ways to rule with minimal interference. This shift set the stage for the monumental changes of the 16th century, including the English Reformation under Henry VIII and Elizabeth I, but those lie in our future chapters.

8.13 Summary of Chapter 8

The late Middle Ages in England were shaped by the personal rule of Richard II, who lost his throne through misjudgments and tyranny, and by the Lancastrian kings who followed. Henry V's glorious victories in France offered fleeting hopes of a dual monarchy, but under Henry VI, the English position collapsed. Internal power struggles escalated into the Wars of the Roses, a dynastic contest between Lancaster and York. The conflict's rapid shifts, betrayals, and fierce battles devastated many noble families.

Out of this turmoil, Henry Tudor, a distant Lancastrian claimant, emerged victorious at Bosworth Field, founding the Tudor dynasty in 1485. His accession marked the end of medieval political chaos and the beginning of a more centralized monarchy. Socially and economically, this period saw the continued decline of strict feudalism, the growth of English as a literary and administrative language, and the rise of a more confident sense of English identity, partly forged through conflict with France.

Having covered the essential developments up to 1485, we now move toward the final stages of medieval England's transformation. In subsequent chapters, we will see how the Tudors harnessed new religious and political currents, steering the country into a different age. But for now, the Wars of the Roses' end and Henry VII's coronation stand as a major pivot point, concluding the medieval era and laying foundations for early modern Britain.

Chapter 9: The Tudor Era – Reformation and Exploration (1485–1558)

Introduction

By 1485, Henry Tudor had seized the English throne at the Battle of Bosworth Field, ending the Wars of the Roses and founding the Tudor dynasty. His accession introduced a new stage in England's history. Under the Tudors, the kingdom experienced crucial religious changes, severing ties with the Roman Catholic Church and establishing the Church of England. Royal power grew more centralized, commerce expanded, and early voyages of discovery hinted at England's rising global ambitions. Though overshadowed at times by religious conflict, the Tudor era reshaped nearly every aspect of English life, laying the foundations for the transformations of the 16th and 17th centuries.

This chapter explores the reigns of Henry VII, Henry VIII, Edward VI, and Mary I, leading up to Elizabeth I's accession in 1558. We will consider how the monarchy reasserted order after civil war, how new economic policies and maritime ventures emerged, and how religious tensions played out in dramatic shifts between Protestantism and Catholicism. By the end of this chapter, we will see how England, once a country scarred by internal conflict, stood ready to begin forging an overseas empire, even as it wrestled with its own spiritual identity.

9.1 Henry VII: Consolidation After the Wars of the Roses

When Henry VII (reigned 1485–1509) defeated Richard III at Bosworth, he ended decades of civil unrest between the Lancastrian and Yorkist factions. However, his grasp on power remained tenuous. Several Yorkist claimants and pretenders appeared over the years, threatening to revive the conflict. Henry countered them by forging strategic alliances and employing careful financial and dynastic policies:

1. **Dynastic Security**: To strengthen his position, Henry married Elizabeth of York, uniting the red rose of Lancaster with the white rose of York. This symbolic marriage helped reduce factional rivalries. He also worked to eliminate or neutralize potential threats. Pretenders like Lambert Simnel

and Perkin Warbeck found support among disaffected nobles or abroad. Yet Henry's intelligence network and diplomatic skill enabled him to capture these threats and secure relative stability.

2. **Financial Reforms**: Henry recognized that a strong treasury would give him independence from overmighty nobles and from frequently summoning Parliament for funds. He enforced royal dues, fines, and feudal rights rigorously, sometimes controversially. The Court of the Star Chamber pursued cases involving powerful nobles who might otherwise escape local justice. These policies boosted royal income but often alienated those forced to pay stiff penalties.

3. **Diplomatic Marriages**: To keep foreign threats in check, Henry arranged marriages for his children that would yield alliances. His eldest son, Arthur, married Catherine of Aragon, daughter of the powerful Spanish monarchs Ferdinand II of Aragon and Isabella I of Castile. This Anglo-Spanish tie promised mutual defense against France. After Arthur's untimely death in 1502, Henry secured papal dispensation for Catherine to marry his second son, Prince Henry—later Henry VIII—further preserving the Spanish alliance.

4. **Merchant Support and Trade**: Under Henry VII, England pursued commercial treaties to expand the cloth trade, especially in the Low Countries. The Merchant Adventurers, a prominent group of English traders, grew in influence. Henry also dabbled in early exploration: he commissioned John Cabot, who sailed from Bristol and reportedly reached North America's coast (likely Newfoundland) in 1497. Though overshadowed by Spanish and Portuguese voyages, this venture hinted at England's future seafaring ambitions.

By the time Henry VII died in 1509, he left a more stable and solvent kingdom than he had inherited. His cautious style and meticulous bookkeeping gave the monarchy greater control over the realm, setting the stage for the more dramatic changes of his son's reign.

9.2 Henry VIII: Early Reign and the Break with Rome

Henry VIII (reigned 1509–1547) inherited a full treasury and a relatively peaceful realm. Initially popular, the young king embodied the Renaissance spirit. He was athletic, well-educated, fluent in multiple languages, and eager for glory in warfare and diplomacy. Yet Henry's early successes gradually gave way to an all-consuming quest for a male heir, which ultimately led him to break from the Roman Catholic Church.

1. **Initial Policies and Cardinal Wolsey**: During the early years of Henry's rule, real power often rested with Cardinal Thomas Wolsey, who served as Lord Chancellor and papal legate. Wolsey orchestrated diplomatic maneuvers, building alliances with various European states. He also oversaw legal reforms and lavish displays of royal prestige, such as the Field of the Cloth of Gold summit with Francis I of France in 1520. These events showcased England's emerging prominence on the European stage.
2. **The King's "Great Matter"**: Henry VIII's marriage to Catherine of Aragon produced only one surviving child, Princess Mary (born 1516). Henry longed for a male heir to secure the Tudor succession. Convinced that God withheld sons from him due to his marriage to his deceased brother's widow, Henry sought an annulment. Pope Clement VII, however, was reluctant to grant this due to Catherine's royal Spanish connections and the political pressures from her nephew, Emperor Charles V. Wolsey failed to secure the annulment, leading to his downfall.
3. **Supremacy and Schism**: Frustrated by papal intransigence, Henry turned to radical measures. Under the guidance of Thomas Cromwell and Thomas Cranmer, he declared himself Supreme Head of the Church of England through the 1534 Act of Supremacy. This severed ties with Rome, allowing Henry to marry Anne Boleyn. The Dissolution of the Monasteries followed, with monastic lands and wealth confiscated by the Crown. While some welcomed the break—especially those influenced by Protestant ideas—many remained faithful to Catholicism and resented the destruction of religious houses that had provided charity and community services.
4. **Multiple Marriages and Succession Anxiety**: Henry married six times in his quest for a stable line of heirs. Anne Boleyn bore him Elizabeth (the future Elizabeth I) but fell out of favor and was executed. Jane Seymour gave birth to a long-awaited son, Edward, but died soon after. Henry's subsequent marriages—to Anne of Cleves, Catherine Howard, and Catherine Parr—reflected more political maneuvers and personal complexities. By the end of his life, Henry named his son Edward as heir, with Mary and Elizabeth to follow if Edward died childless.

Henry's break with Rome fundamentally altered England's religious and political landscape. Although Henry's own personal beliefs remained closer to traditional

Catholicism than to radical Protestant reform, his assertion of royal re
authority paved the way for further doctrinal changes under his succ

9.3 Religious and Cultural Impacts of Henry VIII's Reforms

The dissolution of monasteries between 1536 and 1540 was arguably the most immediate and visible outcome of Henry's Reformation. Hundreds of monastic communities, some centuries old, were disbanded. Their lands, libraries, and treasures were seized. While this boosted the Crown's finances, it also redistributed vast tracts of property to nobles and gentry who bought up former church estates at bargain prices, thus creating new alliances in favor of the Tudor regime.

- **Social Consequences**: Monasteries had offered social services like caring for the poor, travelers, and the sick. Their closure disrupted these functions. Some monastic lands were turned into grand country estates, fueling the rise of powerful local gentry. Others were left to ruin. A wave of iconoclasm (the destruction of religious images) also swept parts of the country, though Henry's personal preferences remained fairly traditional.
- **Pilgrimage of Grace**: Not all the realm accepted these changes calmly. In 1536, northern counties revolted in what became known as the Pilgrimage of Grace. Rebels demanded the restoration of monasteries and the removal of Cromwell. Although Henry offered negotiations, the rebellion was ultimately crushed, and key leaders were executed. It showed that the Reformation, at least in its early form, was far from universally embraced.
- **Humanism and Learning**: Henry's court was influenced by Renaissance humanism. Scholars like Sir Thomas More and Erasmus had earlier promoted the study of classical texts. More's refusal to acknowledge Henry as Supreme Head of the Church led to his execution, exemplifying how intellectual debates about the Church's role turned deadly under Henry's harsh enforcement of loyalty.

By the time of Henry VIII's death in 1547, England had transformed socially, politically, and religiously. Henry left behind a kingdom uncertain about its own faith, but one in which the Crown had demonstrated unprecedented power.

4 The Reigns of Edward VI and Mary I: Swinging Pendulum of Religion

After Henry VIII's death, his nine-year-old son, Edward VI, ascended the throne. Under Edward, Protestant reformers gained significant ground. However, Edward's short reign ended in 1553, paving the way for Henry's Catholic daughter, Mary, to reverse these changes. The period became a tumultuous cycle of religious experimentation and retrenchment.

1. **Edward VI (1547-1553)**:
    - **Regency Government**: Because Edward was a minor, real power lay with his uncles, first Edward Seymour (Duke of Somerset) and later John Dudley (Duke of Northumberland). Both regents pushed for more radical Protestant reforms than Henry VIII had allowed.
    - **Book of Common Prayer**: Archbishop Thomas Cranmer introduced the Book of Common Prayer (1549, revised 1552), simplifying worship and removing many Catholic elements. Traditional religious practices, like the veneration of saints and elaborate church decorations, were discouraged or banned.
    - **Economic Hardships**: Alongside religious changes, economic struggles deepened. Inflation, poor harvests, and social unrest led to rebellions such as Kett's Rebellion in 1549. The regency tried to manage these crises, but faced widespread dissatisfaction.
    - **Succession Crisis**: Fearing Mary's Catholicism, the Duke of Northumberland convinced Edward to name Lady Jane Grey, a Protestant cousin, as heir. After Edward's death in 1553, Jane was proclaimed queen for just nine days before Mary's supporters overthrew her.
2. **Mary I (1553-1558)**:
    - **Return to Catholicism**: Upon taking the throne, Mary quickly restored communion with Rome, repealing Edward's Protestant legislation. She married Philip of Spain (future Philip II), hoping to secure a Catholic alliance and produce an heir to keep England Catholic.
    - **Persecution of Protestants**: Mary's regime burned around 280 Protestants at the stake for heresy, including Cranmer, Ridley, and Latimer. This earned Mary the grim nickname "Bloody Mary" from Protestant chroniclers.

- **Foreign Policy Woes**: Mary's involvement in her husband's war against France led to the loss of Calais, England's last stronghold on the continent. This further damaged her popularity.
- **Lack of an Heir**: Despite multiple phantom pregnancies, Mary never produced a child. She died in 1558, leaving the throne to her half-sister, Elizabeth, who would swing the nation back toward Protestantism.

Edward VI's policies had carried England further down the path of the Reformation, while Mary I attempted to yank the nation sharply back to Catholicism. The rapid shifts caused widespread confusion and fear. Many people were simply relieved when Mary died without entangling the kingdom in further foreign conflicts. Yet these convulsions meant England in 1558 was in desperate need of stability—spiritually, economically, and diplomatically.

9.5 Tudor Exploration and Maritime Ventures

While religious drama dominated the headlines, Tudor monarchs also supported maritime exploration and privateering:

- **Henry VII's Sponsorship**: John Cabot's voyages in 1497 and 1498, financed partly by Bristol merchants, gave England a brief claim to parts of North America. Although Henry VII did not fully capitalize on these discoveries, the precedent of Atlantic navigation was set.
- **Henry VIII's Navy**: Henry VIII expanded the royal navy, building dry docks at Portsmouth and establishing the navy as a professional force. He commissioned great ships like the Mary Rose, which sank in 1545 but demonstrated evolving naval technology.
- **Private Ventures Under Edward and Mary**: Though overshadowed by religious turmoil, merchants and adventurers like Sebastian Cabot (John's son) and merchants of the Muscovy Company sought northern routes to Asia or engaged in trade with Russia, the Baltic states, and the Mediterranean.
- **Elizabeth's Legacy Emerges**: Even before Elizabeth I took the throne, a class of adventurous seamen, motivated by profit and national pride, was taking shape. Figures like John Hawkins and Francis Drake would soon rise to prominence. These early maritime efforts laid the groundwork for what would become a more robust English exploration policy in the

Elizabethan age, though it was still limited compared to Spanish or Portuguese exploits.

9.6 Economic and Social Developments

Alongside religious and exploratory endeavors, the Tudor era saw significant shifts in agriculture, commerce, and social hierarchy:

1. **Enclosure Movement**: As wool exports grew more lucrative, landowners in some areas converted arable fields into pasture for sheep. This process, known as enclosure, displaced traditional peasant communities and sparked local resistance. Parliament debated enclosure repeatedly, revealing tensions between peasant rights and landowner profits.
2. **Rise of a New Gentry**: The Dissolution of the Monasteries allowed well-off commoners and lesser nobles to buy church lands cheaply. This fueled the emergence of a more influential gentry class, loyal to the Crown that had facilitated their rise in wealth.
3. **Urban Growth**: London's population surged, driven by trade and the Tudor court's presence. Other towns, such as Norwich, Bristol, and York, developed specialized industries in textiles or overseas commerce. Guilds continued to regulate trades, though changing economic conditions sometimes strained traditional guild structures.
4. **Cultural Flourishes**: The Renaissance spirit influenced music, art, and education among the elites. Henry VIII prided himself on music composition; his court attracted scholars and artists. Grammar schools multiplied, offering more widespread (though still elite) literacy. Oxford and Cambridge universities expanded their curricula, introducing humanist and Protestant ideas that would shape future church leaders.

By the mid-16th century, England had become more populous, commercially active, and culturally vibrant, despite the strain of religious upheavals. The seeds for overseas trade and exploration were planted, and an increasingly literate gentry could engage in governance. But England had also endured violent swings from Catholic to Protestant rule, with each monarch imposing religious conformity. As Mary I's reign ended in 1558, many wondered how Elizabeth I would address these deep divides.

9.7 The Accession of Elizabeth I (1558)

When Mary I died childless, her half-sister Elizabeth, daughter of Henry VIII and Anne Boleyn, became queen. Elizabeth's father's break with Rome and her mother's tragic fate made her a polarizing figure to staunch Catholics. However, her intelligence, political caution, and Tudor bloodline gave her a claim that many were prepared to accept after years of turmoil.

Elizabeth inherited a kingdom weakened by war with France, saddled with debt, and deeply fractured by religious conflict. Yet her coronation in 1559 was greeted with widespread relief. People longed for a stable government that could heal religious divisions and avoid entangling England in costly foreign wars.

By the time Elizabeth ascended the throne, the English Reformation had progressed too far to be undone, yet Catholic sympathies still ran strong in parts of the country. The path Elizabeth would choose—one of moderate Protestantism, avoiding the extremes of either side—would be central to her early efforts. Her reign, which would last nearly 45 years, laid the bedrock for England's eventual emergence as a major European power, setting the stage for the cultural and political transformations described in the next chapter.

9.8 Summary of Chapter 9

The Tudor era from 1485 to 1558 was defined by dramatic shifts in government, religion, and overseas ambition:

- **Henry VII** rebuilt royal finances and ended lingering civil conflicts.
- **Henry VIII** broke with Rome to secure a male heir, creating the Church of England and confiscating monastic lands. This centralization of authority, combined with Protestant influence, shook traditional religious life to its core.
- **Edward VI** advanced Protestant reforms further, only for **Mary I** to restore Catholicism and launch severe persecutions.
- Meanwhile, maritime exploration and naval growth laid groundwork for future overseas expansion, while economic changes saw the enclosure movement reshape the countryside and a wealthier gentry class rise to prominence.

By 1558, the nation was desperate for stability. Elizabeth I's accession promised a chance to mend rifts, consolidate England's gains, and forge a new balance in religious policy. The next chapter will focus on her reign, the Elizabethan Age, and the cultural vibrancy that produced figures like William Shakespeare—an era that would leave a lasting mark on English identity and prestige.

Chapter 10: The Elizabethan Age and Cultural Flourish (1558–1603)

Introduction

Elizabeth I's reign (1558–1603) is remembered as a golden age of English history. The queen deftly navigated religious divisions, consolidated her power through careful court management, and oversaw a cultural flowering that included renowned writers, dramatists, and poets. She also faced formidable challenges: threats from powerful Catholic monarchies abroad, rebellions at home, and the ongoing uncertainty of the royal succession. England became more assertive at sea, supporting maritime ventures that undercut Spanish power and opened new trade routes. In this chapter, we will explore Elizabeth's religious settlement, her courtly culture, the drama of plots and rebellions, the intensification of exploration, and the cultural achievements that still shape perceptions of the "Elizabethan Age."

10.1 The Elizabethan Religious Settlement

Upon taking the throne, Elizabeth I acted swiftly to resolve religious tensions. She aimed for a middle path—often called the "via media"—that retained enough traditional elements to calm moderate Catholics but affirmed Protestant doctrines to satisfy reformers.

1. **Act of Supremacy (1559)**: This act restored the monarch as Supreme Governor of the Church of England. The title "Supreme Governor" (instead of "Head") offered a slight diplomatic concession, implying the monarch was not claiming absolute spiritual authority. Nonetheless, it reasserted independence from Rome.
2. **Act of Uniformity (1559)**: A revised Book of Common Prayer was introduced, blending the more Protestant 1552 version with some more conservative wording. Attendance at Anglican services became compulsory. People who refused risked fines or worse, yet Elizabeth rarely enforced the harshest penalties—she wanted compliance rather than martyrdom.

3. **Moderation vs. Extremism**: Elizabeth allowed certain Catholic vestiges, like vestments and some ceremonial practices, to remain. However, she placed strict limits on open Catholic worship. Radical Protestants—later called Puritans—agitated for a more thorough reformation. While Puritans criticized the Queen's tolerance of "popish" elements, Catholics lamented the loss of full communion with Rome. Elizabeth's government targeted Catholic recusants who refused to attend Anglican services, but large-scale persecutions like Mary's burnings were not repeated.

This settlement became the enduring foundation of the Church of England, balancing Protestant doctrine with ceremonial continuity. Although tensions remained, Elizabeth managed to avoid the wide-scale religious conflicts that plagued some other European states.

10.2 Challenges to Elizabeth's Rule: Plots and Rebellions

Despite her popularity, Elizabeth I confronted numerous domestic and international threats:

1. **Mary, Queen of Scots**: Catholic Mary Stuart posed the greatest dynastic challenge. After being forced to abdicate the Scottish throne, Mary sought refuge in England in 1568. Elizabeth, wary that Mary's claim to the English throne could inspire Catholic plots, kept her under house arrest for nearly two decades. Multiple conspiracies attempted to replace Elizabeth with Mary, culminating in the Babington Plot (1586). Reluctantly, Elizabeth signed Mary's death warrant in 1587, removing a focal point for Catholic rebels but also fueling international outrage.
2. **Northern Rebellion (1569)**: Disgruntled northern earls, who remained staunchly Catholic, rose against Elizabeth, hoping to free Mary Stuart and restore Catholic worship. The rebellion failed, and Elizabeth responded with harsh punishments. This event underscored lingering Catholic loyalties in the north and the Crown's readiness to crush dissent.
3. **Papal Excommunication (1570)**: Pope Pius V issued the bull Regnans in Excelsis, excommunicating Elizabeth and absolving her subjects of loyalty. This action emboldened Catholic plotters but ultimately did not spur a mass uprising. Instead, it hardened Elizabeth's resolve to monitor and curb Catholic activities.
4. **Puritan Critiques**: On the Protestant side, Puritans challenged Elizabeth's moderate reforms, labeling them half-measures that retained too much

"popish" ritual. Some Puritans sought to purify the Church entirely. Elizabeth resisted drastic changes, defending the settlement as best for national unity. Conflicts with Puritan leaders over vestments and church structure simmered throughout her reign, though Puritans remained a minority.

In navigating these threats, Elizabeth employed a robust network of spies and informants, often orchestrated by her spymaster Sir Francis Walsingham. This covert approach prevented many plots from materializing into open rebellion, securing the Queen's position despite external and internal conspiracies.

10.3 Foreign Policy and the Spanish Armada

England's rivalry with Catholic powers, especially Spain, shaped much of Elizabeth's foreign policy. While she tried to avoid open war, repeated clashes involving trade, piracy, and religious allegiances made conflict almost inevitable.

1. **Support for Protestant Causes**: Elizabeth provided covert support to Protestant rebels in the Netherlands, which were under Spanish rule. English privateers—often with the Crown's tacit approval—attacked Spanish shipping in the Atlantic. The most famous among these "sea dogs" was Sir Francis Drake, who raided Spanish ports in the Americas and seized valuable bullion cargoes.
2. **The Armada (1588)**: Infuriated by English interference and piracy, King Philip II of Spain prepared a massive naval invasion—la "Gran Armada." Composed of around 130 ships, the Armada aimed to transport a Spanish army from the Netherlands to invade England. However, the English fleet, benefiting from more maneuverable ships and better gunnery, scored early successes in the Channel. Then, a storm (later called the "Protestant Wind" by jubilant English Protestants) scattered the Armada as it tried to circumnavigate the British Isles. Many Spanish vessels were lost on the rocky coasts of Scotland and Ireland. The invasion thus failed decisively.
3. **Aftermath and Ongoing Conflict**: While the Armada's defeat was not the end of Anglo-Spanish hostilities, it proved a turning point. Spain remained a formidable power, but England's naval reputation soared. Elizabeth capitalized on the triumph, portraying her reign as divinely favored. Smaller English expeditions continued raiding Spanish interests, and Spain attempted more naval expeditions, though none matched the scale of 1588.

The Armada victory not only safeguarded England from a potential Catholic takeover but also stoked national pride. It underscored the importance of maritime power, signaling that England could punch above its weight in European affairs.

10.4 Elizabethan Exploration and Overseas Ventures

During Elizabeth's reign, seafaring became a crucial dimension of English ambition. Motivated by profit, national pride, and the desire for new trade routes, English sailors embarked on daring voyages:

1. **Privateering and Piracy**: Before formal colonies, many English expeditions operated in a legal gray area. Adventurers like John Hawkins engaged in the transatlantic slave trade, while others attacked Spanish possessions in the Caribbean. Elizabeth tacitly encouraged these activities to undermine Spain's wealth from the New World.
2. **Francis Drake's Circumnavigation**: In 1577, Drake set out on a voyage that took him across the Atlantic, around South America's Cape Horn, up the Pacific coast, and across the Indian Ocean, returning to England in 1580. He brought back treasure looted from Spanish settlements, delighting Elizabeth, who knighted him aboard his ship, the Golden Hind. His circumnavigation demonstrated England's growing naval capabilities.
3. **Colonial Beginnings**: Attempts to establish permanent colonies in North America began under Elizabeth's patronage. Sir Walter Raleigh sponsored expeditions to Roanoke Island in present-day North Carolina (1585–1587), aiming to form the "Cittie of Raleigh." Although these efforts ultimately failed—the "Lost Colony" famously vanished—such projects were precursors to later settlements in Virginia and New England during the 17th century.
4. **The East India Company (1600)**: Right at the twilight of Elizabeth's reign, she granted a royal charter to the East India Company, enabling merchants to trade in the East Indies. Though small at first, the Company would grow into a significant player in global commerce, laying groundwork for a future British Empire.

Elizabeth's selective sponsorship of these ventures reflected her cautious approach: encouraging exploration that might bring wealth and prestige without over-committing Crown resources to uncertain colonies. Nonetheless, the seeds of a global trading network had been planted.

10.5 The Elizabethan Court and Cultural Splendor

Elizabeth built a courtly environment famous for its pageantry, patronage, and intellectual life. Courtiers vied for the Queen's favor through poetry, masques, and displays of loyalty:

1. **Royal Progresses**: Elizabeth embarked on regular "progresses," traveling with her household to various noble estates, forcing wealthy hosts to lavishly entertain her. This practice helped the Queen keep an eye on her subjects, reduce her personal expenses, and project royal magnificence across the kingdom.
2. **Court Factions**: Powerful figures like Sir William Cecil (Lord Burghley), Robert Dudley (Earl of Leicester), Sir Francis Walsingham, and later Robert Devereux (Earl of Essex) competed for influence. Elizabeth adeptly balanced these factions, ensuring none dominated too greatly. Royal favor could make or break a noble's career, so courtiers engaged in elaborate flattery and intrigue.
3. **Patronage of the Arts**: Elizabeth and her leading courtiers sponsored writers, musicians, and artists. Portraiture became popular, with court painters like Nicholas Hilliard producing miniature likenesses. Music flourished as composers like William Byrd navigated the fine line of religious politics while writing both Catholic and Anglican church pieces, as well as secular songs.

This courtly culture cultivated an atmosphere that prized wit, creativity, and display, contributing directly to the literary and artistic achievements for which the Elizabethan age is renowned.

10.6 Elizabethan Literature and Drama

One of the most enduring legacies of Elizabeth's reign is the explosion of literary talent. The emergence of public theaters, combined with increasing literacy among the gentry, fostered a vibrant cultural scene:

1. **The Theater Scene**: Purpose-built playhouses like The Theatre (opened in 1576), The Curtain, The Rose, and The Globe appeared around London. Playwrights wrote both for court entertainments and these commercial

stages, reaching a wide social audience. Gentlemen, merchants, and even laborers often mingled at performances, though their seating varied according to class.
2. **William Shakespeare (1564–1616)**: Shakespeare stands out as the era's most famous dramatist. Born in Stratford-upon-Avon, he arrived in London by the 1590s. Writing for the Lord Chamberlain's Men (later the King's Men), he produced comedies, histories, and tragedies such as A *Midsummer Night's Dream*, *Henry V*, *Hamlet*, and *Macbeth*. His works blended humanist learning, classical influences, and deep insight into human nature, appealing across social strata.
3. **Contemporaries**: Christopher Marlowe's bold plays, like *Doctor Faustus*, challenged moral and religious boundaries. Ben Jonson, a slightly later figure, would refine comedic satire. Poets such as Edmund Spenser (*The Faerie Queene*) celebrated national identity and royal virtue. Sir Philip Sidney's sonnets and prose romances also exemplified Renaissance courtly literature.
4. **Impact on Language**: Elizabethan dramatists and poets enriched English vocabulary, inventing words, phrases, and idioms still in use. The King James Bible (authorized in 1604, completed in 1611) was a bit later but grew from the era's literary ethos, shaping modern English expression. Thanks to these authors, literary English attained a stature comparable to the great vernacular traditions on the continent.

This literary golden age was inseparable from Elizabeth's courtly milieu, which rewarded eloquence and wit. Writers found patrons among the aristocracy and royal officials, while public demand for entertainment made theater a profitable enterprise.

10.7 Late Reign Challenges: The Earl of Essex and Factional Strife

As Elizabeth aged, she faced difficulties maintaining the same level of control over factions:

1. **Robert Devereux, 2nd Earl of Essex**: A dashing courtier who rose to prominence in the 1590s, Essex enjoyed Elizabeth's favor but clashed with Lord Burghley's son, Sir Robert Cecil. Sent to quell rebellion in Ireland, Essex failed to achieve quick victory, then returned to court without permission—a serious breach of royal protocol. In 1601, he led a short-lived rebellion in London, hoping to gain control of the queen and

force changes in her government. The plot collapsed, and Essex was executed.
2. **Ireland and Tyrone's Rebellion**: Ireland remained a thorn in Elizabeth's side. Hugh O'Neill, Earl of Tyrone, led a major uprising (Nine Years' War, 1594–1603). Spanish support intermittently arrived, viewing Ireland as a strategic way to pressure England. Essex's failure there heightened tensions. Eventually, Lord Mountjoy replaced Essex and managed to contain the revolt, though at great cost in men and money.
3. **Succession Anxiety**: Elizabeth refused to name a direct heir, publicly at least. Many assumed that James VI of Scotland (Mary Stuart's son) would succeed, as he was the nearest Protestant relative. However, Elizabeth deliberately withheld official endorsement, using the uncertainty to keep her court in line. Anxiety about the future sometimes fueled factional maneuvering.

These final years saw Elizabeth's once-brilliant court become weary and fractious, especially after long wars and mounting debts. Nonetheless, she remained a popular figure, often hailed as "Good Queen Bess," especially among those who feared renewed instability if she died without a smooth succession.

10.8 Elizabeth's Death and the End of an Era

Elizabeth died on 24 March 1603 at Richmond Palace. Her passing marked the end of the Tudor dynasty's direct line, as she left no children. Yet the transition to James VI of Scotland—who became James I of England—was relatively peaceful, reflecting the behind-the-scenes arrangements among advisors.

Under Elizabeth, England had navigated religious schism, repelled a massive Spanish invasion, and fostered a cultural renaissance. Although the kingdom was still far from modern democracy or industrial power, it had achieved a degree of unity and identity absent a century earlier. Parliament had grown more influential, seafaring had expanded English horizons, and literature had reached astonishing new heights. The Elizabethan Age's mystique, blending courtly elegance with dramatic achievements in exploration and the arts, would cast a long shadow over subsequent generations.

10.9 The Legacy of the Elizabethan Age

In retrospect, Elizabeth's long reign shaped countless aspects of English history:

1. **Religious Stability**: The Elizabethan Settlement laid foundations for the Anglican Church, enabling it to endure beyond the Tudor period despite future internal disputes. The notion of a moderate Protestantism, reflecting national identity, became firmly embedded.
2. **Growth of National Consciousness**: Victories like the defeat of the Spanish Armada fueled patriotic sentiments. Writers glorified England's "sceptered isle," while explorers championed the kingdom's maritime destiny.
3. **Cultural Prestige**: The creative outpouring of drama, poetry, and prose during Elizabeth's reign gave English literature a global reputation. Shakespeare, Marlowe, Spenser, and others remain central to the English literary canon.
4. **Imperial Aspirations**: Although England was not yet the major colonial power it would become, Elizabeth's seafarers took the first steps toward building overseas footholds. The East India Company charter and early North American attempts presaged a more aggressive colonial policy in the 17th century.
5. **Myth and Symbol**: Elizabeth's image as the Virgin Queen who sacrificed personal happiness for her realm became a potent national myth. Subsequent monarchs, including James I and Charles I, would find it difficult to match her iconic status.

With Elizabeth's death, the stage was set for the Stuart era. England would soon face new controversies over royal prerogative, religious dissent, and constitutional governance. But the Tudor period's achievements, especially under Elizabeth, remained vivid in the national memory, often idealized as a golden age of strong monarchs, vibrant culture, and growing national confidence.

10.10 Summary of Chapter 10

The Elizabethan Age (1558–1603) stands out for its religious compromise, cultural brilliance, and the growing sense of English identity that emerged under Queen Elizabeth I:

- **Religious Settlement**: Elizabeth tread a careful path between Catholic and Protestant extremes, cementing Anglicanism as England's state religion.
- **Plots and Political Intrigue**: Catholic conspiracies and Puritan challenges tested Elizabeth's government. Mary, Queen of Scots, remained a figurehead for Catholic discontent until her execution in 1587.
- **Foreign Conflicts**: Tension with Spain culminated in the Spanish Armada's defeat in 1588, boosting national pride and England's naval reputation.
- **Exploration and Maritime Ventures**: Privateering, circumnavigation by Drake, and early colonial attempts signaled England's future rise as a seafaring power.
- **Cultural Flourish**: Shakespeare and his contemporaries transformed English drama, while courtly patronage encouraged poetry, music, and painting, forming a cultural legacy still revered today.

By the close of Elizabeth's reign, England was more secure, cohesive, and outward-looking than at any point since the Norman Conquest. Although many challenges lay ahead, the final Tudor monarch left a lasting imprint on the kingdom's sense of itself and its prospects in the wider world.

Chapter 11: The Stuarts and the English Civil War (1603–1649)

Introduction
When Queen Elizabeth I died in 1603, she left no direct heir. The throne passed to the Stuart line in Scotland, uniting the crowns of England and Scotland under James VI of Scotland, who became James I of England. This new dynasty faced a host of challenges: religious division remained a powerful force in the kingdom, financial problems strained the Crown's resources, and questions about the proper balance of power between monarch and Parliament lingered. Over the next decades, these issues would intensify, culminating in open conflict known as the English Civil War. Ultimately, the war ended with the unprecedented trial and execution of King Charles I in 1649. This chapter explores how a monarchy that seemed so strong under the Tudors encountered such devastating turmoil under the Stuarts.

11.1 The Accession of James I

James I (James VI of Scotland) inherited the throne after Elizabeth I's death in March 1603. He was the son of Mary, Queen of Scots, and had become King of Scotland while still a child. England greeted James with a mixture of curiosity and relief: curiosity, because he was a king from a different realm who held certain Presbyterian ideas; relief, because his succession averted a contested claim that might have led to further conflicts. James, for his part, hoped to unify England and Scotland more closely, though he did not formally merge them during his reign.

James's Beliefs on Kingship
James believed firmly in the "divine right of kings," holding that monarchs derived authority directly from God, not from the people. He wrote treatises, such as *The True Law of Free Monarchies*, explaining his philosophy that a king was like a father to his people and should not be challenged by Parliament. However, he also realized he needed to work with the political structures in England, including Parliament, to secure funds and cooperation. Elizabeth had left the Crown in debt, so James's desire to reign without much parliamentary interference quickly ran into practical problems.

Hopes and Disappointments

Many English Puritans expected James to push the Church of England toward a more Protestant, "Calvinist" style of worship and governance, especially given Scotland's Presbyterian tradition. However, James maintained the Episcopal system (with bishops) of the Church of England. He clashed with Puritan demands at the Hampton Court Conference (1604), famously declaring "No bishop, no king." He feared that weakening the role of bishops might also weaken monarchical authority. Some moderate reforms were introduced, such as commissioning the King James Bible (published 1611), which became a literary landmark, but more radical Puritans felt let down.

11.2 The Gunpowder Plot and Catholic Tensions

Religious tensions went beyond Puritan dissatisfaction. Catholics had endured penalties under Elizabeth I, and while James initially reduced some fines for recusants (those who refused to attend Anglican services), overall Catholic hopes for full toleration were dashed. The infamous Gunpowder Plot of 1605 arose from a small group of Catholic conspirators led by Robert Catesby, including Guy Fawkes. They aimed to blow up the House of Lords during the State Opening of Parliament, intending to kill James, his family, and leading Protestants, then incite a Catholic uprising.

Discovery and Aftermath

Authorities discovered the plot just in time. Fawkes was found guarding barrels of gunpowder in a cellar beneath Parliament. The plotters were arrested, tortured, and executed. This event solidified anti-Catholic sentiment in England, making Catholicism seem synonymous with treason. Laws against Catholics grew stricter, and the monarchy and Parliament joined in condemning any perceived Catholic threat. James's desire to find a balance between harsh repression and a degree of toleration was further complicated by widespread fear of popish conspiracies.

11.3 Financial Struggles and the Early Parliament Disputes

Throughout James I's reign, money remained a contentious issue. The Crown's finances were drained by the costs of maintaining the royal household, foreign policy, and the inflated court culture James encouraged. In Scotland, James had grown accustomed to a smaller budget and tried to import some Scottish favorites into the English system. English courtiers resented these newcomers, who received titles and pensions. Parliament, for its part, was reluctant to approve new taxes without concessions from the king.

The Great Contract (1610)
An ambitious attempt to settle royal finances was called the Great Contract, proposed by James's chief minister, Robert Cecil (Earl of Salisbury). Under it, Parliament would grant James a fixed annual sum to cover expenses, while James would give up certain feudal dues and prerogatives. Negotiations collapsed over mutual distrust and disagreements. This failure meant that the Crown limped along financially, relying on outdated systems of feudal revenue, customs duties (impositions), and forced loans.

Rise of Favorites
As James struggled to secure revenues through Parliament, he came to rely more on favorites at court, such as Robert Carr (Earl of Somerset) and later George Villiers (Duke of Buckingham). These men became extremely influential in guiding royal policy and patronage, stirring jealousy among the old nobility. Parliamentary members disliked the sense that decisions were being made by unqualified favorites instead of responsible ministers. Tensions between Crown and Parliament simmered, although no outright crisis erupted while James lived.

11.4 Charles I Inherits the Throne

James I died in 1625, leaving the throne to his second son, Charles I. (James's elder son, Henry Frederick, had died young in 1612.) Charles was more reserved than his father, and he shared James's strong belief in the divine right of kings. He also had close ties to the Duke of Buckingham, inheriting him as a favorite. Almost immediately, Charles faced a foreign policy disaster in a failed expedition against Spain, which Parliament blamed on Buckingham's mismanagement. Parliament withheld funds and criticized Buckingham openly. Charles, in turn, felt Parliament was overstepping its authority.

Marriage and Religious Outlook
Charles's marriage to the French Catholic princess Henrietta Maria further alarmed English Protestants, who feared Catholic influence at court. Although Charles promised not to grant major concessions to Catholics, rumors circulated about secret pro-Catholic sympathies. Meanwhile, within the Church of England,

Charles favored a High Church approach, supporting bishops like William Laud who promoted more ceremonial worship. Many Puritans saw this as a drift back toward Catholic-style practices.

11.5 Parliament vs. King: Early Flashpoints

Between 1625 and 1629, Charles summoned and dissolved Parliament multiple times in quick succession. Each time, disputes over taxes and royal authority escalated:

1. **Forced Loans**: Parliament was unwilling to grant Charles substantial funds for his war aims. Desperate for revenue, Charles resorted to forced loans—essentially compelling wealthy subjects to lend him money. Those who refused risked imprisonment. This move caused outrage among MPs and the gentry, who viewed it as illegal without parliamentary consent.
2. **Petition of Right (1628)**: Eventually, Parliament agreed to grant subsidies if Charles addressed grievances. They drafted the Petition of Right, declaring that the king could not levy taxes without parliamentary approval or arbitrarily imprison subjects. Although Charles accepted the petition under duress, he quickly tried to sidestep its spirit.
3. **Assassination of Buckingham (1628)**: The unpopular Duke of Buckingham was assassinated by a disgruntled soldier, John Felton. Many in Parliament celebrated, believing Buckingham was a main cause of corruption and failed policies. Charles, however, was deeply grieved, blaming the climate of hostility stirred by Parliament for Buckingham's death.
4. **Personal Rule (1629–1640)**: Furious that Parliament persisted in criticizing his policies, Charles dissolved it in 1629 and did not call another for eleven years. This period is sometimes called the "Eleven Years' Tyranny" by critics, though Charles himself thought it was a lawful exercise of his prerogative. He governed without Parliament, raising money through obscure fees like ship money and expanding the roles of royal courts. Tensions festered as many feared for their rights and for the Protestant faith under bishops like Laud.

11.6 Religious Conflict and the Road to War

During Charles's Personal Rule, Archbishop William Laud tried to impose uniform worship practices across England and Scotland. In England, Laud's reforms included beautifying churches, insisting on strict observance of the Book of Common Prayer, and punishing Puritan preachers who resisted. But perhaps the biggest flashpoint emerged in Scotland, where Laud and Charles attempted to enforce a new prayer book. Scots, who had a strong Presbyterian tradition, violently rejected these measures.

The Bishops' Wars (1639–1640)
Scotland rose in revolt, signing the National Covenant (1638) to defend their religion against what they saw as an Anglican invasion. Charles attempted to put down the rebellion but lacked funds for a proper army. With no Parliament to grant money, Charles was forced to summon first the Short Parliament in 1640, which he dissolved after just three weeks when it demanded redress of grievances before granting funds. Needing resources to fight the Scots, he was ultimately forced to call a new Parliament—the Long Parliament—in November 1640.

Long Parliament's Assertiveness
The Long Parliament, led by men like John Pym, seized the opportunity. They impeached Archbishop Laud and Thomas Wentworth (Earl of Strafford), Charles's key advisor, for high treason. Strafford was executed in 1641. Parliament passed laws making it illegal for a king to dissolve them without their own consent, ensuring Parliament could not be dismissed as easily as before. They also abolished the Star Chamber, a symbol of arbitrary royal justice. By late 1641, tensions were at boiling point, with both sides suspecting the other of radical intentions.

11.7 Outbreak of the Civil War

Amid these anxieties, rumors circulated that Charles was secretly negotiating with Catholic forces or planning a coup. In January 1642, Charles attempted to arrest five leading members of Parliament on charges of treason. This direct assault on parliamentary privilege failed—the Five Members had been warned and fled. Mobs in London turned hostile, and Charles fled the capital. Both Parliament and King began raising armies, each claiming to defend the "true" constitution.

Royalists and Parliamentarians

The country split into those loyal to the king (Royalists or Cavaliers) and those supporting Parliament (Parliamentarians or Roundheads). Many nobles and country gentry supported Charles out of loyalty or fear of social upheaval. Other landowners, merchants, and Puritan groups aligned with Parliament, fearing Charles aimed for absolute power or a Catholic restoration. War officially began in 1642 when the king raised his standard at Nottingham.

11.8 Major Phases of the English Civil War

Historians often divide the conflict into several phases:

1. **First Civil War (1642–1646)**: Initial battles favored the king's experienced cavalry. Notable engagements included Edgehill (1642) and Marston Moor (1644). Over time, Parliament reorganized under the leadership of figures like Oliver Cromwell, whose New Model Army emphasized discipline and strong Puritan morale. By 1646, Charles was forced to surrender, seeking refuge with the Scots.
2. **Divisions Among the Victors**: Even after Charles's capture, Parliament was split between moderates (Presbyterians) who wanted a negotiated settlement with the king, and radicals (Independents) who demanded more fundamental changes. Meanwhile, the Scots, who had aided Parliament, expected the imposition of Presbyterianism across England. Charles tried to exploit these divisions by negotiating separately with each faction.
3. **Second Civil War (1648)**: Charles's secret dealings with the Scots led to a brief Second Civil War. Royalist uprisings flared in parts of England and Wales. The New Model Army swiftly crushed these rebellions. Furious at Charles's duplicity, many in the army concluded there could be no lasting peace while he lived. This shift in attitude set the stage for Charles's trial.

11.9 The Trial and Execution of King Charles I

At the end of 1648, the army expelled from Parliament those members who still favored negotiation, in an event known as Pride's Purge. Left behind was the Rump Parliament, dominated by hardline Independents. They established a High Court of Justice to try Charles for treason against his own people. Charles refused to recognize the court's authority, claiming kings answered only to God. Nevertheless, he was found guilty and sentenced to death.

Execution and Shock

On 30 January 1649, Charles I was beheaded outside the Banqueting House in Whitehall. This act stunned Europe: an anointed monarch executed by his own subjects was unprecedented in England. Royalists saw it as regicide, while radicals claimed it was necessary to uphold the people's liberty against a tyrant. A wave of pamphlets, sermons, and debates followed, justifying or condemning the act. With Charles dead, England was declared a Commonwealth, abolishing the monarchy and the House of Lords. Thus ended the first major stage of the Stuart crisis, but the next years would bring their own upheavals.

11.10 Social and Cultural Dimensions of the Civil War

The Civil War was not solely a top-level political struggle. It affected towns, villages, and families across the realm:

1. **Local Divisions**: Some communities split along personal or religious lines. Others tried to remain neutral, suffering plunder from whichever side arrived. Commerce and agriculture suffered disruption, though the war was not as continuously destructive as conflicts in continental Europe.
2. **Religious Radicalism**: The breakdown of censorship during the war allowed various religious sects—Baptists, Quakers, Fifth Monarchists, and others—to spread their ideas. Soldiers in the New Model Army, many of whom were zealous Protestants, debated theology and politics in camp. A ferment of radical thought questioned social hierarchies and challenged established norms.
3. **Role of Women**: Women sometimes managed estates or participated in defense of their homes when male family members were away fighting. Some women also engaged in political petitioning, addressing Parliament on issues such as high prices or injustice toward prisoners. Although they did not gain formal political power, the war allowed certain women to step out of traditionally passive roles.
4. **Press and Propaganda**: Pamphlets, news sheets, and sermons flourished, with each faction trying to shape public opinion. This was one of the earliest periods of widespread use of print propaganda in England, setting precedents for modern media strategies.

11.11 Consequences and Significance

By 1649, the centuries-old tradition of monarchy in England seemed shattered. No king, no House of Lords, and a radical Parliament in power—this was a profound constitutional shift. The war had exposed deep fault lines between Crown and Parliament, as well as within society over religion, governance, and personal freedoms. Although the monarchy would eventually be restored, the Civil War's legacy endured. It planted ideas of contractual government, parliamentary sovereignty, and the possibility of challenging royal authority in the public mind. For many, the war also displayed the grim cost of discord and fanaticism: tens of thousands died, property was destroyed, and communities were torn apart.

In the short term, power passed to a Commonwealth and, eventually, to Oliver Cromwell's Protectorate. Yet the division between those seeking a godly republic and those longing for a return to monarchy and Church stability did not vanish overnight. Debates over tolerance, representation, and the nature of English government continued unabated. The next chapter will examine the Commonwealth under the Rump Parliament, Cromwell's rise, and the eventual Restoration of the Stuart line under Charles II. But the path leading to that Restoration was anything but straightforward.

11.12 Summary of Chapter 11

From 1603 to 1649, England saw a dramatic transformation in its political and religious life under the early Stuarts:

- **James I** brought together the crowns of England and Scotland, championed divine right, and struggled with parliamentary finances.
- **Charles I** intensified conflicts over taxation and religion, leading to multiple dissolutions of Parliament and an eleven-year Personal Rule.
- Attempts to impose uniform worship in Scotland sparked revolt, forcing Charles to recall Parliament. The Long Parliament curbed his powers, and mutual mistrust erupted into the **English Civil War** (1642–1646).
- Parliament's New Model Army defeated royal forces, capturing Charles. His maneuvers triggered a brief **Second Civil War** in 1648.

- Radical MPs and army officers placed Charles on trial for treason, resulting in his execution in January 1649.

The monarchy's collapse shocked Europe, leaving England a republic under parliamentary rule, at least nominally. While the conflict settled immediate questions of authority, deeper issues about governance, faith, and rights remained unresolved. Thus ended the first great Stuart crisis, shaping a legacy of questioning royal power that would resonate into future generations.

Chapter 12: The Commonwealth and the Restoration (1649–1660)

Introduction

The death of Charles I in January 1649 opened a new and uncertain chapter in English history. For the first time, the realm had neither king nor House of Lords, and was instead declared a Commonwealth, ruled by the remaining members of Parliament—the Rump Parliament—and its army allies. Over the next decade, leadership shifted from parliamentary committees to the forceful presence of Oliver Cromwell, whose Protectorate tried to establish a "godly" government. This period, known collectively as the Interregnum, witnessed continuing wars in Ireland and Scotland, the rise of radical religious groups, and attempts at constitutional reform. Ultimately, however, dissatisfaction with Puritan austerity and military rule led many to welcome back the monarchy in 1660 under Charles II. This chapter explores the twists and turns of the Commonwealth and Protectorate, culminating in the Restoration settlement that reversed many of the revolutionary changes of 1649.

12.1 Establishing the Commonwealth (1649–1653)

After Charles I's execution, the Rump Parliament abolished the monarchy and the House of Lords, proclaiming England a Commonwealth. It declared itself the supreme authority, backed by the New Model Army. Many questions loomed: Would the Commonwealth endure, or was it a temporary experiment until a new settlement arose? Could it unite a divided nation still reeling from civil war?

1. **Rump Parliament's Agenda**: The Rump attempted to govern through committees and ordinances. It pursued reforms in law, though progress was slow. One notable success was the Navigation Act of 1651, aimed at bolstering English maritime commerce by restricting foreign (particularly Dutch) ships from carrying goods to England or its colonies unless they originated from the carriers' home countries. This act would eventually spark conflict with the Dutch.
2. **Challenges to Legitimacy**: Many royalists refused to recognize the Commonwealth. Some moderate parliamentarians were appalled that

their peers had executed the king. Even among the revolutionaries, factions arose, such as the Levellers, who demanded broader suffrage, religious toleration, and rights like equality before the law. The Rump Parliament, wary of radical democracy, crushed Leveller mutinies in the army, imprisoning or silencing their leaders like John Lilburne.

3. **Wars in Ireland and Scotland**: In Ireland, large sections of the population remained loyal to the monarchy or were motivated by Catholic solidarity against the Protestant-dominated Commonwealth. Cromwell led a brutal campaign in 1649–1650, capturing strongholds like Drogheda and Wexford, where atrocities were committed against defenders. In Scotland, royalist sentiments grew around Charles II (son of the executed king), who was proclaimed king by Scottish Covenanters in 1649. The Commonwealth faced the prospect of renewed war in the north.

12.2 Cromwell's Rise to Power

Oliver Cromwell, a skilled commander from the Civil Wars, rose as the central figure in the Commonwealth's military and political life. Though he initially supported the Rump, Cromwell grew frustrated with its slow pace of reforms and its reluctance to schedule new elections. He believed England needed a more "godly reformation," not endless parliamentary wrangling.

Dissolving the Rump

In April 1653, Cromwell forcibly dissolved the Rump Parliament, storming into the chamber with soldiers. He allegedly declared, "You have sat too long for any good you have been doing lately," dismissing the members. This abrupt move ended any pretense that the Commonwealth was purely parliamentary. In its place, Cromwell summoned a handpicked assembly of religious reformers, nicknamed the Barebone's Parliament (after one of its members, Praise-God Barebone). However, this group soon proved unwieldy and surrendered power back to Cromwell by year's end.

12.3 The Protectorate (1653–1658)

In December 1653, a new constitution called the Instrument of Government declared Oliver Cromwell Lord Protector. England, Scotland, and Ireland were united under this single regime. This arrangement created a system of checks and balances: Cromwell as Protector, a Council of State, and parliaments elected under new rules. In reality, Cromwell held most of the power, backed by the army.

1. **Religious Policies**: Cromwell, an Independent, favored broad Protestant toleration (except for Catholics and extreme sects he saw as dangerous). He ended compulsory use of the Book of Common Prayer, allowing various Protestant congregations some freedom. Jewish resettlement in England was tacitly permitted. Yet strict moral codes were enforced, discouraging theater, popular festivals, and other amusements deemed sinful.
2. **Military Rule**: To suppress potential uprisings, Cromwell divided England into eleven regions, each governed by a major-general. These major-generals, drawn from the army, enforced Puritan moral regulations and collected taxes. This system was deeply unpopular among the gentry and merchants who disliked military interference in civilian affairs.
3. **Foreign Ventures**: Cromwell pursued an ambitious foreign policy. He continued the war with the Dutch, which ended in 1654. Then he challenged Spain, seeking to expand English influence in the Caribbean. The Western Design expedition (1655) captured Jamaica, establishing a foothold that would become a significant English colony. Cromwell also formed alliances with Protestant states on the continent, hoping to elevate England's status as a leading Protestant power.
4. **Parliamentary Conflicts**: Cromwell summoned parliaments under the Protectorate, but relations were tense. Many MPs wanted to reduce the army's power or restore some form of traditional monarchy. Others opposed Cromwell's tolerant stance on religion or disliked the high taxes needed to support the military. Cromwell dissolved these parliaments when they challenged him, underscoring his reliance on personal authority and the threat of force.

12.4 Offer of the Crown and Cromwell's Refusal

In 1657, a new constitution called the Humble Petition and Advice was presented to Cromwell, which would have made him King. Many of his advisers believed a monarchy, even with a different name, offered stability and tradition. Yet Cromwell hesitated. Having fought a war against what he saw as monarchical tyranny, accepting the crown might alienate his base of army officers and radical supporters. Ultimately, he refused the title, remaining Lord Protector. However, the revised constitution did grant him the right to name his successor, effectively creating a quasi-hereditary system.

12.5 The Death of Oliver Cromwell and the Collapse of the Protectorate

Oliver Cromwell died in September 1658. His son, Richard Cromwell, inherited the title of Lord Protector. But Richard lacked his father's commanding presence and political skill. The army quickly lost confidence in him, and financial problems mounted. After a few months, Richard resigned, and the Protectorate began to unravel.

Return of the Rump
In 1659, senior army officers reinstalled the Rump Parliament, attempting to govern without a Protector. This arrangement pleased almost no one. Radical soldiers, Presbyterians, royalists, and disaffected gentry all vied for control. General George Monck, commanding forces in Scotland, emerged as a key power broker, deciding that restoring stable governance required recalling the MPs purged in 1648. This effectively undid Pride's Purge and allowed for the possibility of inviting Charles II to return.

12.6 The Restoration of the Monarchy (1660)

Sensing the widespread yearning for order, Monck marched south, orchestrating negotiations. In early 1660, the so-called Convention Parliament, freely elected without the strict controls of the Interregnum, assembled. They welcomed the Declaration of Breda from Charles II, in which he promised amnesty, religious leniency, and back pay for the army if recalled as king. This Parliament voted to restore the monarchy, House of Lords, and the Church of England in its earlier form.

Charles II's Triumphant Return
Charles II landed at Dover in May 1660 to cheering crowds. The monarchy was back, though some changes remained—many of the old feudal dues were not reinstated, and Parliament had a stronger sense of its importance. Charles II took a conciliatory stance, famously declaring he would forgive past offenses

except those who directly participated in his father's execution. Several regicides were tried and executed, including some already dead whose bodies were exhumed and symbolically punished. The Restoration thus signaled an official condemnation of the "rebellion" and a desire to move forward under a reestablished king.

12.7 Life Under the Restoration

While the monarchy returned, the Restoration was not merely a reversion to the pre-war status quo:

1. **Religious Settlement**: Charles II reinstated the Anglican Church as the state religion under bishops. The Clarendon Code (1661–1665) penalized dissenters (those who refused the Book of Common Prayer, including Presbyterians, Independents, and Baptists). Catholics also faced discrimination. Despite Charles's private leanings toward religious toleration, political pressures led him to maintain policies that favored the Church of England.
2. **Political Landscape**: Parliament remained suspicious of royal absolutism. The era's constitutional balance was more complex than before the civil wars, as MPs retained the power of the purse. Charles's finances, though improved by grants, never made him fully independent of Parliament. The memory of 1649 discouraged any king from ignoring or dissolving Parliament for long stretches.
3. **Social and Cultural Changes**: The Restoration Court was notorious for its hedonism, contrasting sharply with Puritan austerity. Theaters reopened, women appeared on stage as actresses for the first time, and playwrights like William Wycherley and John Dryden produced witty comedies. Science also flourished; the Royal Society, founded in 1660, promoted empirical research and included figures like Robert Boyle and Isaac Newton (though Newton's major works came slightly later).
4. **Lingering Divisions**: Under the surface, old resentments persisted. Some extreme Protestants felt betrayed that their dream of a godly republic was crushed. Royalists cheered the triumphant monarchy but remained worried about the potential for future uprisings. The uneasy settlement set the stage for ongoing tensions that would flare in the reigns of Charles II and James II, culminating in further transformations by the end of the 17th century.

12.8 Ireland and Scotland During the Interregnum and Restoration

The civil wars and Interregnum had profound consequences for Ireland and Scotland, as well:

- **Ireland**: Cromwell's conquests devastated large areas. Land confiscations punished Catholic landowners, redistributing property to English and Protestant settlers. After the Restoration, Charles II restored some lands to royalist loyalists, but many dispossessed Catholics never recovered their estates. Tensions over land, religion, and English dominance remained high, sowing seeds of future conflict.
- **Scotland**: Initially, Scotland had crowned Charles II in 1651. After Cromwell's armies defeated the Scots at Dunbar (1650) and Worcester (1651), Scotland came under direct rule from London, its parliament dissolved. At the Restoration, Scotland regained its separate parliament and institutions, though Charles II demanded adherence to episcopacy in the Scottish Church, sparking future strife with Covenanters.

12.9 Radical Groups and Their Fate

Many radical sects that flourished in the 1640s and 1650s found themselves suppressed by the Restoration regime:

1. **Quakers**: Originating with George Fox, Quakers promoted pacifism, equality, and an inner "Light of Christ." They faced imprisonment and fines for refusing to swear oaths or attend Anglican services, but continued to grow underground.
2. **Fifth Monarchists**: Believing in the imminent reign of King Jesus on Earth, they tried and failed to seize power under Cromwell, and launched a small uprising after Charles II returned. The rebellion was crushed, and the group faded.
3. **Levellers**: Their push for popular sovereignty and expanded suffrage had been repressed even before Cromwell's death. Under the Restoration, Leveller ideals inspired future democratic movements, but as an organized force they no longer existed.

12.10 The Legacy of the Commonwealth and Restoration

Despite lasting only 11 years (1649–1660), the Commonwealth and Protectorate eras left deep marks on England's political culture. They showed that the monarchy could be overthrown—and that it could be restored. Parliamentary authority had grown, with the recognized power to shape taxation and question the Crown. The experience of a Puritan-led government also influenced religious life, making many English people wary of extremes in either direction.

The Restoration, though it revived the monarchy and Anglican Church, did not erase memories of the Civil War. Royal authority was tempered by fears of stirring old conflicts, and Parliament's voice remained strong. Religious dissenters were suppressed but did not disappear. Over the next decades, these tensions would feed into new struggles over James II's Catholicism and the question of a Protestant succession, culminating in the events of 1688–1689 (the Glorious Revolution). But for now, the Restoration era under Charles II signaled that the nation wanted normalcy after years of upheaval.

12.11 Daily Life and Cultural Shifts

For ordinary people, the Interregnum and Restoration brought both change and continuity:

- **Economy**: Agricultural practices continued evolving, with enclosure proceeding steadily. Trade expanded, boosted by the Navigation Acts and growing maritime power. London's population kept rising, becoming a hub for commerce and a magnet for rural migrants seeking work.
- **Gender and Family**: Puritan ideals had briefly emphasized moral discipline, patriarchal authority, and close family structures. The Restoration did not drastically alter family life, but the renewed prominence of courtly fashions and amusements provided alternative social models for the elite.
- **Scientific Curiosity**: Cromwell's relative openness to new ideas, followed by Charles II's patronage, encouraged scientific discussions. The Royal Society, chartered in 1662, fostered experiments and the exchange of knowledge. Though not every English person directly experienced these developments, they heralded a shift toward empirical reasoning that would characterize the Enlightenment.

- **Press and Information**: Restrictions on printing fluctuated, but overall the civil wars had spurred growth in pamphleteering. By the Restoration, the appetite for news, plays, and published works had not diminished. Periodicals started to appear, a trend that would grow in the late 17th and early 18th centuries.

12.12 Conclusion and Transition to the Late Stuart Period

With Charles II restored to the throne in 1660, England nominally resumed its traditional monarchy. Nonetheless, the experiences of civil war, regicide, and Commonwealth rule had profoundly altered the political landscape. Parliament had proven it could challenge and even eliminate a king. Radical religious and political movements left an undercurrent of dissent. The Restoration settlement offered short-term stability, but questions about the ultimate balance of power between Crown and Parliament—and about religious toleration—remained.

Moving Forward
The later years of Charles II's reign and the succession of his brother, James II, would bring these unresolved tensions to the forefront. Fears of a Catholic monarch and a return to absolutism led to renewed crises, culminating in the Glorious Revolution of 1688–1689, which replaced James II with William and Mary under conditions that guaranteed parliamentary power. However, those developments belong to another phase of English history. For our purposes, the Restoration of 1660 stands as the endpoint of the great Stuart upheavals we have followed since 1603. The monarchy, once shattered by civil war, had returned, but forever changed. England now entered a period of ongoing negotiation between royal authority, parliamentary rights, and diverse religious communities—a legacy that would shape the nation for centuries to come.

12.13 Summary of Chapter 12

From 1649 to 1660, England experimented with republican government under the Commonwealth and Oliver Cromwell's Protectorate:

- **Rump Parliament** declared a Commonwealth, grappling with legitimacy issues and wars in Ireland and Scotland.

- **Cromwell** rose as Lord Protector in 1653, instituting a military-backed regime that allowed some religious freedom for Protestants but stifled cultural amusements and heavily taxed the population for a strong army.
- **Foreign Policy** aimed at boosting England's trade and Protestant alliances, leading to conflict with the Dutch and Spanish.
- **The Protectorate** ended with Cromwell's death in 1658; his son Richard was unable to hold power, and factional chaos ensued.
- **General Monck's Intervention** restored a free Parliament, which invited **Charles II** to return in 1660, marking the **Restoration** of the monarchy.

Though the Stuart monarchy was reestablished, the events of the Interregnum had permanently changed the political and religious landscape. Parliament's power grew, certain radical ideas persisted underground, and the Crown learned to proceed with more caution. This era's upheaval and eventual compromise highlight how deeply monarchy and parliament shaped each other, setting the stage for further developments before modern times.

Chapter 13: The Glorious Revolution and the Early Georgian Era (1660–1714)

Introduction

The Restoration of King Charles II in 1660 brought a sense of relief and renewed monarchy to the realm, but it did not settle all the underlying tensions laid bare by the Civil Wars and Interregnum. The latter decades of the 17th century saw the monarchy's relationship with Parliament continue to evolve—and often clash—over issues of religious toleration, royal prerogative, and the succession. These tensions reached a critical point during the reign of James II, resulting in the so-called "Glorious Revolution" of 1688–1689, which permanently changed the constitution by asserting Parliament's supremacy over certain royal claims. After this seismic shift, England (and later Great Britain, after the 1707 union with Scotland) entered the rule of the early Georgian monarchs, beginning with George I in 1714. During this period, the foundations of modern parliamentary democracy were further strengthened, religious toleration expanded for some groups, and Britain established itself as a growing imperial and commercial power in Europe and beyond.

This chapter will detail how the Restoration monarchy navigated repeated crises, culminating in James II's deposition and the replacement of the Catholic Stuart line with the Protestant William III and Mary II. We will also examine the subsequent reign of Queen Anne and the transition to the Hanoverian dynasty under George I, setting the stage for the significant social, economic, and colonial changes explored in the following chapter.

13.1 Charles II: Challenges After the Restoration

When Charles II returned to London in May 1660, the monarchy and the Anglican Church were officially restored. However, these institutions did not pick up exactly where they had left off in 1642. Over a decade of upheaval had changed England in fundamental ways:

1. **Constitutional Shifts**:
    - Although the Crown regained broad powers, Parliament had demonstrated its capacity to control taxation and exert real pressure on the monarch.

- There was general agreement that no future king should attempt to rule without Parliament for long periods, as Charles I had done.
2. **Religious Controversies**:
    - Charles II was outwardly Anglican, but rumors of his private Catholic leanings persisted.
    - The Clarendon Code (1661–1665) established strict penalties for religious dissenters (Presbyterians, Baptists, Quakers, and others) who refused conformity to the Church of England.
    - Despite Parliament's anti-dissenter stance, Charles sometimes sought ways to relax laws against Catholics and Protestant nonconformists—partly due to his own sympathies and partly to maintain civil peace.
3. **Restoration Culture**:
    - The court became known for its lively atmosphere. Theaters reopened, actresses performed on stage for the first time in English history, and playwrights like John Dryden composed witty comedies of manners.
    - Scientific inquiry flourished under the aegis of the Royal Society (chartered in 1662), attracting minds like Robert Hooke, Robert Boyle, and later Isaac Newton (whose major works appeared in the 1680s).
4. **Foreign Policy and Finance**:
    - Wars with the Dutch continued, partly fueled by naval rivalry and trade competition, and partly by Charles's desire to assert maritime power.
    - Parliaments were reluctant to grant Charles large financial resources. This forced him into sometimes-questionable alliances, including a secret treaty with France (the Treaty of Dover, 1670), in which he promised to consider converting to Catholicism and assist France against the Dutch, in exchange for subsidies from Louis XIV.

The Great Plague of 1665 and the Great Fire of London in 1666 added to the sense of a tumultuous era. Even so, the economy and population rebounded fairly quickly, with London undergoing major rebuilding. By the 1670s, the stage was set for a new wave of political conflict, especially focusing on religion and succession.

13.2 The Exclusion Crisis and the Popish Plot

A central source of tension during Charles II's reign concerned the line of succession. Charles had no legitimate children who survived; thus, his brother James, Duke of York, was next in line. James had converted to Catholicism, a fact that alarmed a Protestant political nation still wary of "popish" influences. Parliamentarians and pamphleteers often portrayed Catholicism as synonymous with political tyranny, citing parallels to Louis XIV's absolute monarchy in France.

1. **Popish Plot (1678)**:
    - Titus Oates, a disreputable Anglican clergyman, claimed to have uncovered a vast conspiracy by Catholics to assassinate Charles II and place James on the throne.
    - Public hysteria ensued, leading to arrests and executions. While the supposed "Popish Plot" was largely fabricated, it tapped into real paranoia about Catholic infiltration.
2. **Exclusion Crisis (1679–1681)**:
    - The so-called Whig faction in Parliament tried to pass the Exclusion Bill, seeking to bar James, Duke of York, from the throne.
    - The Tory faction defended the principle of legitimate succession and the king's prerogative, warning that excluding James would upend monarchical stability.
    - Charles II, outraged at Parliament's attempt to manipulate the succession, dissolved Parliament multiple times and relied on Tory support. The Exclusion efforts ultimately failed.

Whigs and Tories emerged during this crisis as the beginnings of England's modern political party system, though their platforms were still fluid. By the time Charles II died in 1685, the succession crisis had not been resolved by legislation. James, Duke of York, succeeded without immediate resistance—becoming James II.

13.3 James II and the Path to Revolution

James II (r. 1685–1688) confirmed many people's worst fears by promoting Catholic interests openly. His reign began with some popular sympathy—he vowed to uphold Anglican dominance while advocating limited toleration for Catholics. However, James soon took a series of steps that alienated broad swaths of his subjects:

1. **Rebellion and Royal Response**:
   - The Monmouth Rebellion (1685): James Scott, Duke of Monmouth, an illegitimate son of Charles II, attempted to raise a revolt in the West Country, styling himself a Protestant alternative to James II. The rebellion was crushed, and James II oversaw harsh punishments known as the "Bloody Assizes," led by Judge Jeffreys.
2. **Religious Declarations**:
   - James II issued the Declaration of Indulgence (1687), suspending the penal laws against both Catholics and Protestant dissenters. On the surface, this might have appealed to those seeking greater toleration, but it was widely perceived as a unilateral, illegal assertion of royal power, bypassing parliamentary statute.
   - James further placed Catholics in high office, ignoring statutes that excluded them. He clashed with the Anglican clergy by demanding they read his Declaration of Indulgence from their pulpits.
3. **Fear of a Catholic Dynasty**:
   - James's second wife, Mary of Modena, gave birth to a son in June 1688, raising the specter of a permanent Catholic Stuart dynasty. Until then, many Protestants had comforted themselves with the knowledge that James's older daughters, Mary and Anne—both raised Protestant—were next in line. A male heir overturned that assumption.

At this point, leading English statesmen, both Whig and Tory, decided they could not endure James's Catholic policies any longer. They issued a secret invitation to William of Orange (Stadtholder of the Dutch Republic and husband of James's Protestant daughter, Mary) to intervene. William, who was already engaged in conflict with Louis XIV of France, recognized an opportunity to secure England's support in his continental wars.

13.4 The Glorious Revolution (1688–1689)

In November 1688, William of Orange landed in southwest England with a sizeable army. James II, panicked by desertions among his officers and the general hostility of his subjects, fled London. After an attempt to regroup, he eventually escaped to France. William did not claim the throne outright by conquest; instead, a Convention Parliament was summoned to determine the succession. In early 1689, Parliament offered the crown jointly to William and Mary on the condition they accept the Declaration of Rights (later enacted as the Bill of Rights).

1. **Bill of Rights (1689)**:
    - Asserted that monarchs could not suspend laws or levy taxes without parliamentary consent.
    - Reaffirmed the right of subjects to petition, bear arms (for Protestants), and enjoy freedom from cruel and unusual punishments.
    - Established that the monarch must not be or become Catholic and that Parliament should be called frequently.
2. **Significance**:
    - The "Glorious Revolution" was relatively bloodless in England (though not in Ireland or Scotland), thus earning its name.
    - It cemented the principle of a constitutional monarchy, where the king or queen governed in partnership with Parliament, subject to law.
    - The Toleration Act (1689) allowed many Protestant dissenters the freedom to worship, though full political rights remained restricted. Catholics still endured severe legal disabilities.

Though "glorious," the revolution did not instantly create a fully democratic system. Power remained concentrated among the landed classes, and Parliament was not widely representative of the entire population. Still, the settlement of 1689 laid a lasting foundation that limited royal authority more systematically than ever before.

13.5 William III and Mary II: Securing the Revolution Settlement

William III and Mary II (r. 1689–1694 jointly; William alone until 1702) spent much of their reign consolidating the new constitutional arrangement and confronting foreign threats—particularly from Louis XIV of France, who offered refuge to James II and supported Jacobite rebellions (those favoring the exiled Stuarts). Key issues included:

1. **War with France**:
    - The Nine Years' War (1688–1697) pitted William III and the Grand Alliance against Louis XIV's expansionist ambitions. England's

resources were heavily committed, which in turn necessitated stronger parliamentary cooperation to fund the war effort.
    - This ongoing need for parliamentary financing strengthened legislative oversight, leading to more regular sessions of Parliament.
2. **Jacobite Threats**:
    - The most notable Jacobite uprising during William's reign was in Scotland, where supporters of James II mounted resistance, resulting in battles like Killiecrankie (1689). The movement lingered, especially among Highland clans and in Ireland, where James II had briefly tried to recapture his throne in 1689–1690, culminating in William's victory at the Battle of the Boyne (1690).
    - Jacobitism persisted as a political force, with supporters periodically attempting to restore the "rightful" Stuart line.
3. **Administrative and Financial Reforms**:
    - Under William, institutions like the Bank of England (founded 1694) were established to manage the debt incurred by continuous warfare, reflecting the growing complexity of public finance.
    - A permanent national debt and the mechanism of government bonds tied wealthy merchants and bankers to the state, aligning their interests with the Crown-Parliament partnership.

Mary II died in 1694, and William continued to rule alone until his death in 1702. Although William was Dutch and sometimes unpopular among English Tories, his reign solidified the post-revolution structure. He left the throne to Mary's sister, Anne, who would oversee the union of England and Scotland and further entrench the new constitutional order.

13.6 Queen Anne and the Act of Union (1702–1714)

Anne (r. 1702–1714), the last Stuart monarch, was a devout Anglican and popular with many of her subjects. Her reign saw ongoing war in Europe, culminating in the War of the Spanish Succession (1701–1714), as well as significant domestic changes:

1. **Union with Scotland (1707)**:
    - England and Scotland had shared a monarch since James I, but remained separate states with distinct parliaments.

- The Act of Union (1707) created the Kingdom of Great Britain, uniting the two countries under one Parliament in Westminster.
- Scots received representation in the unified Parliament, though some in Scotland resented the deal, feeling they lost sovereignty.
- Economic and political motives—such as guaranteeing the Hanoverian Protestant succession and opening English colonial markets to Scottish merchants—helped drive the union.

2. **War of the Spanish Succession**:
    - This war pitted Great Britain, the Dutch Republic, and other allies against France (and Spain), seeking to prevent the Bourbon family from dominating Spain as well as France.
    - Military figures like the Duke of Marlborough won key victories, notably at Blenheim (1704) and Ramillies (1706). Funding the war demanded repeated parliamentary grants, entrenching the principle that major military campaigns required legislative support.

3. **Rise of Party Politics**:
    - Anne favored Tory advisers initially, but Whigs gained influence as the war progressed, claiming to be more fervent supporters of the Protestant succession and the war effort.
    - Party strife grew intense, with Whigs and Tories contending for control of Anne's affections and appointments. The political "rage of party" shaped parliamentary debates and pamphlet controversies.

4. **Succession Crisis**:
    - Anne had no surviving children (she endured numerous miscarriages and stillbirths). The 1701 Act of Settlement stipulated that if the Stuart line died out, the crown would go to the Protestant descendants of Sophia of Hanover (a granddaughter of James I).
    - This arrangement aimed to prevent any Catholic claimant from taking the throne, thus excluding the direct Catholic Stuarts living in exile.

When Anne died in August 1714, the Stuart line in Britain ended in the sense of direct heirs. The throne passed peacefully to George I of Hanover. This signaled a new phase: the early Georgian era, marked by further entrenchment of parliamentary governance and the continuing development of a global British presence.

13.7 Summary of Chapter 13

From the Restoration in 1660 to the dawn of the Georgian era in 1714, the British monarchy underwent a series of fundamental challenges and transformations:

- **Charles II** navigated a delicate balance between a revived Anglican state and tensions over dissent and potential Catholic sympathies.
- **James II** openly promoted Catholicism, prompting the Glorious Revolution (1688–1689), which replaced him with William III and Mary II under a constitutional framework limiting royal authority through the Bill of Rights.
- **William III** spent much of his reign at war with Louis XIV of France, reinforcing parliamentary cooperation in matters of finance and governance.
- **Queen Anne** oversaw the War of the Spanish Succession, the 1707 union of England and Scotland, and increased the role of party politics in government.
- **Act of Settlement (1701)** and Anne's death (1714) paved the way for the Protestant Hanoverian succession.

The crown was no longer unquestioned in its prerogative; Parliament had firmly established its role in shaping the laws, controlling finances, and deciding succession issues. This new constitutional arrangement provided a platform from which Britain would expand commercially and territorially in the 18th century, as explored in the next chapter.

Chapter 14: Georgian Society, Industry, and Colonial Ambitions (1714–1783)

Introduction

The accession of George I in 1714 inaugurated the Georgian era, spanning the reigns of George I, George II, and George III (with George IV and William IV following later, but beyond our immediate scope). The early-to-mid 18th century witnessed significant shifts in British society, economics, and global reach. With the Glorious Revolution settlement still shaping politics, the Crown found itself increasingly reliant on ministers and parliamentary support. Meanwhile, a burgeoning sense of a British national identity emerged following the Union with Scotland, aided by growing prosperity in commerce, agriculture, and an evolving colonial empire. The period also saw early stirrings of industrial change, even if the full Industrial Revolution would only flourish at the century's end.

This chapter explores how the Hanoverian kings navigated political challenges at home, how British society advanced in areas such as finance, agriculture, and cultural life, and how colonial ventures and conflicts—from North America to India—increasingly defined Britain's global position. We will conclude with the outbreak of the American War of Independence, an event that tested Britain's imperial model and foreshadowed further colonial transformations in the 19th century.

14.1 George I, the Cabinet System, and the Power of Parliament

George I (r. 1714–1727) was a Protestant German prince—Elector of Hanover—who spoke little English. His distant relationship with English politics spurred a shift in governance:

1. **The Growth of Cabinet Government**:
    - Because George I struggled with the language and was more concerned with his Hanoverian interests, he relied on his ministers to manage day-to-day affairs.
    - Sir Robert Walpole emerged as a key figure, effectively becoming the first "Prime Minister" (though not formally called that at the

time). Walpole's long tenure (1721–1742) provided relative stability. He controlled patronage networks, influencing parliamentary votes and policy.
2. **Whigs and Tories**:
   - The early Georgian period saw the Whig Party dominate. They were associated with the Hanoverian succession, the Bank of England, and the trading/financial classes in London.
   - Tories, often linked with landed interests, had been tainted in some eyes by their association with the Jacobite cause—supporting the exiled Stuarts. Over time, Tory fortunes ebbed and flowed, but Whigs generally kept a firm grip on government for decades.
3. **Jacobite Rebellions**:
   - James Francis Edward Stuart ("the Old Pretender") and later Charles Edward Stuart ("Bonnie Prince Charlie") attempted to reclaim the British throne.
   - The 1715 rebellion ("the Fifteen") and the 1745 rebellion ("the Forty-Five") both tested the new Hanoverian regime. The 1745 rising initially had dramatic success in Scotland but ended in defeat at the Battle of Culloden (1746). The failure of these Jacobite efforts effectively ended any serious threat to the Hanoverian line.

With the demise of Jacobitism as a viable political alternative, Britain became more stable under the Hanoverians, consolidating a Whig-dominated parliamentary monarchy.

14.2 Social and Economic Development in the Georgian World

The 18th century brought key transformations to social structures, commerce, and lifestyles:

1. **Agricultural Improvements**:
   - New farming techniques, such as crop rotation (the Norfolk four-course system), selective breeding of livestock, and improved drainage, increased agricultural output.
   - Enclosure continued, replacing open-field systems with more consolidated holdings. This boosted yields but sometimes displaced smaller farmers, who either became wage laborers or migrated to towns.

- A growing rural population found at least partial employment in proto-industrial "cottage industries," like spinning and weaving textiles at home for entrepreneurial clothiers.

2. **Commercial and Financial Expansion**:
   - London served as a major financial center, building on the establishment of the Bank of England and the stock market. Joint-stock companies financed ventures abroad.
   - The South Sea Bubble (1720) was a speculative frenzy surrounding the South Sea Company, which collapsed spectacularly and briefly undermined public confidence. Walpole's skillful management helped Britain recover economically.
   - Regional hubs (Bristol, Liverpool, Glasgow) thrived on trade, including the Atlantic slave trade and the import of colonial goods such as sugar, tobacco, and cotton.

3. **Urban Growth and Social Stratification**:
   - Towns and cities expanded, with new social spaces—coffeehouses, clubs, theaters—serving as centers for news, debate, and leisure.
   - The middle class of merchants, professionals, and tradespeople gained influence, distinguishing themselves from both the aristocracy and the urban poor.
   - Literacy rates gradually climbed, and publishing flourished. Newspapers, journals, and pamphlets circulated widely, fueling discussion of politics, science, and culture.

4. **Cultural Life**:
   - The Georgian era saw notable achievements in the arts and letters. Writers like Jonathan Swift, Daniel Defoe, and Samuel Richardson pioneered new forms of satire and the novel.
   - Architecturally, the Palladian style influenced country houses and public buildings, reflecting a taste for symmetry and classical forms.
   - The Enlightenment currents from continental Europe also influenced British thinkers like David Hume and Adam Smith (though Smith was Scottish, contributing to a broader "British Enlightenment" post-1707).

Overall, the 18th century was a period of relative domestic peace—despite periodic Jacobite risings—enabling Britain to invest in commerce, culture, and empire-building.

14.3 The Empire Expands: North America, the Caribbean, and India

The Georgian period saw Britain aggressively expand its colonial footprint. Several factors contributed:

- **Financial Backing** from joint-stock companies and the state,
- **Naval Dominance** honed by wars with European powers,
- **Trading Networks** including the transatlantic slave trade, linking Africa, the Caribbean, and North America.

1. **North American Colonies**:
    - By the early 1700s, England's mainland colonies stretched along the Atlantic seaboard from New England to the Carolinas and Georgia.
    - These colonies prospered from agricultural exports, including tobacco, rice, and indigo. The Navigation Acts regulated colonial trade to benefit the mother country.
    - Colonists grew used to a degree of self-governance through local assemblies, though they remained under the Crown's ultimate authority.
2. **Caribbean Interests**:
    - Sugar plantations in Jamaica, Barbados, and other islands were major profit centers for British merchants and planters.
    - Enslaved Africans toiled under brutal conditions, generating wealth that flowed back to Britain, fueling further investment and consumer demand for sugar and rum.
3. **The East India Company**:
    - Granted a monopoly over English trade with Asia, the Company established trading posts in India (Madras, Bombay, Calcutta) and further east.
    - Over the 18th century, Company officials extended their influence, forging alliances with local rulers and at times waging war, thus laying the groundwork for future British rule in the Indian subcontinent.
4. **Competing with France**:
    - Britain's chief rival for overseas dominance was France. A series of wars (the War of the Austrian Succession, 1740–1748; the Seven Years' War, 1756–1763) tested each empire's resilience.
    - The Seven Years' War (often called the French and Indian War in North America) ended with a decisive British victory. Britain

gained Canada from France, Florida from Spain (ally of France), and emerged as the leading colonial power in North America.
- This triumph, however, came at a high financial cost, sowing seeds of future conflict over how to pay for the empire's defense.

14.4 Political Leadership under George II and the Rise of George III

George I died in 1727, succeeded by his son George II (r. 1727–1760). Walpole remained the principal minister until 1742, shaping policy and resisting foreign entanglements. Later ministries continued to revolve around Whig alliances, with figures like the Duke of Newcastle and William Pitt the Elder playing major roles, particularly during the Seven Years' War. Key developments include:

1. **Stability and Continuity**:
   - The overall system of parliamentary governance with a prime-ministerial figure in the Commons became more entrenched.
   - George II was more active in British affairs than his father, but he largely accepted the ascendant role of the ministry, provided it delivered results and maintained the Hanoverian interest in Europe.
2. **William Pitt the Elder**:
   - Pitt's leadership from the mid-1750s was crucial in prosecuting the Seven Years' War. He recognized the importance of colonial conflicts and poured resources into the navy and overseas campaigns.
   - His strategies and oratory won him public acclaim, though he clashed with other ministers and George II on expenditures and alliances.
3. **Transition to George III**:
   - George II's grandson, George III (r. 1760–1820), ascended the throne at a relatively young age. He was keen to assert more active royal direction in policy, challenging the powerful Whig factions that had dominated since the early 18th century.

14.5 Society, Science, and the Seeds of Industrial Change

While the full Industrial Revolution is often dated from the late 18th to early 19th century, its forerunners appeared in mid-Georgian Britain:

1. **Early Mechanization**:
    - In textiles, inventors began developing spinning machines (e.g., the "Spinning Jenny" in the 1760s) and water frames. These machines were not yet widespread, but they hinted at the factory system to come.
    - Coal mining expanded to fuel domestic heating, metalworking, and early industrial processes. Steam engine prototypes (Thomas Newcomen's atmospheric engine, early 1700s) were used mainly for pumping water from mines, anticipating James Watt's improvements later in the century.
2. **Enlightenment Influence**:
    - Philosophers and scientists in Britain contributed significantly to Enlightenment thought. Adam Smith's *The Wealth of Nations* (1776) laid the groundwork for classical economics, advocating free trade and the division of labor.
    - Scottish intellectuals (like David Hume) and English polymaths (like Joseph Priestley) advanced fields such as history, chemistry, and moral philosophy.
3. **Social Mobility and Class Tensions**:
    - Some upward mobility was possible for enterprising merchants and inventors, though aristocratic landowners continued to wield immense political power.
    - The poor, both rural and urban, remained vulnerable, relying on charity or parish relief in times of hardship. The Speenhamland system (a late 18th-century phenomenon) would attempt to address poverty by subsidizing wages.
4. **Urban Leisure and Culture**:
    - Coffeehouses and clubs proliferated as hubs for debate, networking, and literary expression. Gentlemen's clubs in London, like White's or Brooks's, became political and social power centers.
    - Popular culture included fairs, pleasure gardens (like Vauxhall), and spectacles such as public balloon ascents (after the 1780s). Despite significant inequalities, a growing consumer society was taking shape.

14.6 Tensions in the American Colonies and the Road to Independence

Britain's success in the Seven Years' War brought enormous new territories in North America (Canada, territory east of the Mississippi), but also a massive war debt. The Crown and Parliament believed the colonies should share the cost of their own defense:

1. **Imperial Reforms**:
   - The Sugar Act (1764), Stamp Act (1765), and Townshend Acts (1767) attempted to raise revenue directly from the colonists, leading to protests about "taxation without representation."
   - Colonists in British America had grown accustomed to local autonomy through their assemblies and objected to parliamentary taxes imposed without their input.
2. **Escalation of Conflict**:
   - Tensions led to riots, boycotts, and the formation of the Sons of Liberty. The Boston Massacre (1770) and Boston Tea Party (1773) became flashpoints.
   - British responses, such as the Coercive Acts (1774), aimed to punish Massachusetts but instead rallied other colonies in solidarity.
3. **Outbreak of War**:
   - Fighting began in 1775 at Lexington and Concord. The Continental Congress declared independence on 4 July 1776, enumerating colonial grievances against King George III in the Declaration of Independence.
   - The war went badly for Britain at times, due to logistical challenges, French intervention on the American side, and a lack of unified strategy.

By 1783, the Treaty of Paris recognized American independence, dealing a severe blow to Britain's global prestige. However, Britain retained Canada and extensive colonial holdings elsewhere. The American crisis forced Britain to reconsider how it managed its empire, leading to reforms in places like Ireland and further caution in dealing with colonies around the world.

14.7 The End of an Era: Britain in 1783

In the wake of the American War of Independence, Britain found itself at a crossroads:

1. **Political Repercussions**:
    - The war's unpopularity weakened Lord North's Tory government, paving the way for a series of short-lived ministries. William Pitt the Younger eventually emerged as a dominant figure from 1783 onward.
    - King George III, though personally affected by the war's failure, remained committed to British interests in Europe and the empire, forging alliances and overseeing gradual economic recovery.
2. **Imperial Shifts**:
    - Despite losing the American colonies, Britain still held a vast network of possessions—including profitable sugar islands in the Caribbean, strategic outposts in India, and growing interests in Australia (where the first penal colony was established at Sydney in 1788).
    - The East India Company's role in India intensified, setting the stage for direct Crown control in the 19th century.
3. **Seeds of Reform**:
    - Intellectuals like Edmund Burke critiqued government excesses and advocated more balanced governance. Calls for the abolition of the slave trade also gained momentum (championed by figures like Granville Sharp, Thomas Clarkson, and later William Wilberforce).
    - Industrial developments, continuing enclosure, and expanding trade laid the groundwork for the dramatic societal changes that would unfold in the late 18th and early 19th centuries.

Thus, by 1783 Britain remained a formidable power—naval, commercial, and increasingly industrial—but it had learned painful lessons about the costs of mismanaging colonial relationships. The American loss would haunt policymakers as they considered future imperial policies elsewhere, even as the home islands advanced in population, capital investment, and technology.

14.8 Summary of Chapter 14

From George I's accession in 1714 to the conclusion of the American War of Independence in 1783, Britain underwent substantial development in governance, society, and empire:

- **Hanoverian Monarchy**:
    - George I's limited engagement in English affairs contributed to the rise of cabinet government under strong ministers like Robert Walpole.
    - Whig dominance and the defeat of Jacobite rebellions stabilized the succession.
- **Economic and Social Growth**:
    - Agricultural improvements, commercial expansion, and early industrial innovations characterized the Georgian era.
    - Cities grew, the middle class expanded, and a flourishing print culture facilitated political debate and cultural exchange.
- **Imperial Ambitions**:
    - Britain emerged victorious in colonial wars against France, securing vast territories in North America, the Caribbean, and beyond.
    - The East India Company entrenched British influence in India, paving the way for later imperial rule.
- **American Rebellion**:
    - The attempt to impose direct taxes on the colonies after the Seven Years' War led to escalating resistance, culminating in the American Revolution.
    - Britain's defeat in 1783 forced a reassessment of colonial governance and contributed to evolving political dynamics at home.

By the early 1780s, Britain was still poised for further growth, but it faced new challenges and uncertainties—both within the British Isles and across its increasingly global empire. The seeds of the Industrial Revolution were sprouting, the call for social reforms was growing, and the stage was set for the 19th century's sweeping transformations. In the next chapters, we will examine how Britain navigated these changes—always keeping our focus on the crucial steps that shaped the United Kingdom before the fully modern era.

Chapter 15: The Road to the Union – Scotland, Ireland, and Wales (1783–1801)

Introduction

By 1783, the United Kingdom of Great Britain was riding the waves of change—having lost its American colonies but retaining significant global interests. The union of England and Scotland, enacted through the 1707 Acts of Union, had already reshaped the political landscape in the northern part of the island. Wales, meanwhile, had been legally annexed in earlier centuries under the Tudor monarchs, although it retained cultural distinctiveness. Ireland posed a more complex situation: it was nominally a separate kingdom, sharing the same monarch as Great Britain but governed by its own parliament in Dublin. Yet tensions—religious, economic, and political—ran high on the island, and events of the late 18th century would lead to the Acts of Union of 1800 (effective 1801), creating the United Kingdom of Great Britain and Ireland.

This chapter investigates how Scotland, Ireland, and Wales navigated pressures from London in the late Georgian era. We will explore the transformations after the Jacobite defeat in Scotland, the rise of new agrarian and cultural trends in Wales, and the explosive situation in Ireland—where sectarian divides and a growing reform movement culminated in rebellion and, ultimately, union with Britain. By 1801, a new constitutional arrangement had taken shape, signaling a further step toward a unified—if still internally diverse—kingdom.

15.1 Scotland After Culloden

The Jacobite Legacy

Following the final defeat of the Jacobite Rising at Culloden (1746), Scotland entered a period of profound social, economic, and political change. Many Highland clans, previously associated with the Stuart cause, found themselves under strict government surveillance. Harsh laws banned the wearing of Highland dress (the tartan kilt), the carrying of arms, and certain forms of Gaelic culture viewed as symbols of rebellion. British military garrisons dotted the Highlands to enforce the new order.

Highland Clearances

Perhaps the most transformative (and traumatic) developments were the so-called Highland Clearances. Beginning in earnest in the later 18th century, landowners—often absentee aristocrats—sought to increase profitability by turning traditional clan-based farming areas into large-scale sheep pastures. Tenant farmers, historically bound by clan ties, were evicted en masse, forcing them to move to coastal regions or emigrate. Some settled in the Lowlands, while many ventured overseas to North America or elsewhere in the empire. The Clearances drastically altered the demographic and cultural landscape of the Highlands, eroding Gaelic language and traditions as communities dispersed.

Economic and Cultural Shifts

Meanwhile, the Scottish Lowlands experienced an intellectual and economic flowering. The Scottish Enlightenment, centered in Edinburgh and Glasgow, produced notable thinkers like Adam Smith, David Hume, and Adam Ferguson. Universities flourished. Merchant wealth in Glasgow grew, due in part to trade in tobacco and other colonial goods. By the end of the 18th century, Scotland's integration within the British framework brought financial opportunities—particularly in banking, commerce, and industry—even as many Highland families suffered dispossession.

Political Integration

Although Scotland had representation at Westminster post-1707, many Scots felt that genuine power lay in London. The Scottish political nation, smaller in number compared to England, often aligned with certain party factions (mainly Whigs) to maintain influence. The expanding empire offered ambitious Scots positions in the civil service, the army, or commerce overseas. Hence, while Scotland retained distinct legal and church institutions—the Scottish law system and the Presbyterian Church—it increasingly participated in Britain's larger imperial and economic ventures.

15.2 Wales in the Late 18th Century

Historical Context

Wales had been legally annexed to the English Crown centuries before, chiefly under the Laws in Wales Acts of 1535 and 1542. By the late 18th century, Wales was fully subject to English law, with no separate Welsh parliament. Yet the Welsh language and cultural identity persisted strongly, especially in rural areas.

The industrializing trends of Georgian Britain began to touch certain parts of Wales—most notably the southern regions containing coal and iron deposits.

Early Industrial Growth
While the truly large-scale industrial transformations would come in the 19th century, the seeds were already visible by 1783. Ironworks sprang up around Merthyr Tydfil and other locales in the South Wales Valleys. Coal mining, though not yet massive, was on the rise, feeding the demands of British factories and households. Migrants from rural Wales or from across the border in England sought work in these emerging industrial areas, beginning a slow but steady process of urbanization.

Religious and Cultural Life
The late 18th century also saw the spread of Nonconformist religious movements in Wales, especially Methodist revivals that inspired large segments of the population. Welsh-language chapel services fostered a sense of communal identity distinct from Anglican England. Hymn-singing traditions grew, and literacy rates improved, in part due to the desire to read the Bible in Welsh. While these developments were not overtly political at this stage, they contributed to a strengthening of Welsh cultural consciousness.

Integration within Britain
Wales, lacking a separate parliament, did not face the same constitutional friction as Scotland or Ireland. It was legally considered part of the Kingdom of England (and, by extension, Great Britain after 1707). However, many Welsh people were concerned about preserving their language and customs in the face of increasing Anglicization. The Georgian era thus witnessed both industrial promise and cultural pride, setting the stage for the 19th-century Welsh revival movements that would assert a more distinct national identity.

15.3 Ireland's Complex Position

Irish Parliament and Sectarian Divides
Unlike Wales, Ireland still had its own parliament, located in Dublin, though in practice it was subordinate to the Westminster government. Since the late 17th century, the so-called Protestant Ascendancy—a small Anglican elite—dominated Irish political, social, and economic life. The vast majority of the population was Catholic or Presbyterian (particularly in the northern province of Ulster) and faced varying degrees of legal discrimination.

Grattan's Parliament

In 1782, under the leadership of Henry Grattan and other reform-minded Protestants, the Irish Parliament won a measure of legislative independence from Britain in what became known as the Constitution of 1782. This "Grattan's Parliament" was hailed as a victory for Irish self-government but did not significantly alleviate the plight of Irish Catholics, who remained excluded from political power by the Penal Laws. Moreover, the Westminster parliament still controlled significant aspects of Irish governance, including trade policy and the executive oversight via the Lord Lieutenant.

Economic Challenges

Ireland's economy was largely agrarian, with much of the land in the hands of absentee landlords living in Britain. Tenant farmers endured high rents and uncertain leases. Export opportunities were hampered by British mercantile regulations that favored the interests of English or Scottish producers. Some small-scale manufacturing existed, particularly in the north (linen production), but for most of Ireland, poverty was rampant. Calls for reform—land reform, Catholic relief, and broader political participation—grew louder, fueled by the spirit of the American and French revolutions.

15.4 The Rise of Irish Nationalism and the 1798 Rebellion

Influence of the French Revolution

The outbreak of the French Revolution in 1789 sent shockwaves through Europe, including Ireland. Radical political ideas—liberty, equality, popular sovereignty—found receptive audiences among both Catholics who sought emancipation and Presbyterians in Ulster who admired republican ideals. In 1791, the Society of United Irishmen was formed in Belfast, advocating parliamentary reform, religious toleration, and, increasingly, the end of British control. Leading figures included Wolfe Tone, Thomas Russell, and others who saw in French republicanism a model for Ireland.

Government Crackdowns

The British administration in Dublin Castle, fearing revolutionary contagion, clamped down on seditious societies. Spies, informants, and harsh penal measures were used to suppress United Irishmen activism. Yet these attempts often backfired, driving the movement underground and radicalizing it further. By the mid-1790s, many United Irishmen favored a fully independent Irish republic.

The 1798 Rebellion

The pivotal moment came in 1798 when open rebellion erupted in several Irish counties. Catholic peasants joined Presbyterian radicals in some regions, though sectarian tensions complicated attempts at unity. The rising was poorly coordinated; hoped-for French military support materialized only weakly and too late. British forces, along with loyalist militias, violently suppressed the insurgents. Thousands died in battles and subsequent retaliations, especially in areas like Wexford. Wolfe Tone, captured after a failed French landing, died in prison—widely regarded as a martyr for Irish independence.

Aftermath and Calls for Union

The 1798 rebellion underscored to British policymakers that Ireland remained dangerously unstable. Prime Minister William Pitt the Younger concluded that a closer political union would provide better security and allow for Catholic emancipation in a controlled manner. Many in the Protestant Ascendancy were also alarmed by the rebellion, fearing that their privilege would be overthrown if French-style revolution took root. Hence, momentum grew for a legislative union, dissolving the Irish Parliament and merging it with that of Great Britain.

15.5 The Acts of Union 1800 and the Creation of the United Kingdom of Great Britain and Ireland

Negotiations and Pressure

In the wake of the rebellion, Pitt's government lobbied Irish parliamentarians to vote for union. Bribery, patronage, and the promise of Catholic relief were heavily employed. Anglo-Irish aristocrats who feared losing influence unless they participated in the union found themselves swayed. Some believed that once union was achieved, the British government would grant Catholic emancipation, giving Catholics a path into the political sphere without the risk of wholesale revolution.

Terms of the Union

The Acts of Union were passed by both the Parliament of Great Britain and the Parliament of Ireland in 1800, taking effect on January 1, 1801. Key provisions included:

1. The Kingdom of Great Britain and the Kingdom of Ireland united into one kingdom, named "The United Kingdom of Great Britain and Ireland."

2. The Irish Parliament was abolished. Ireland would send elected representatives (peers in the House of Lords and MPs in the House of Commons) to Westminster.
3. The Church of Ireland remained established, mirroring the Church of England's status in Britain.
4. Certain trade concessions were made, integrating the Irish economy more directly into the British mercantile system.

Initial Outcomes

While the union ended the nominal independence of the Dublin Parliament, it did not immediately bring Catholic emancipation. King George III, influenced by his coronation oath to uphold the Anglican settlement, opposed granting full civil rights to Catholics. Pitt, who had championed the union partly on the basis of emancipating Catholics, resigned in frustration. Thus, Catholics remained excluded from Parliament and many public offices—a source of continuing grievance that would fuel future agitation (leading to the eventual Catholic Emancipation Act of 1829).

Reactions in Ireland

Reactions were mixed. The Ascendancy class largely supported union, believing it better secured their status. Many Irish Catholics, having been promised relief, felt betrayed when it did not materialize. Economic benefits of union were slow to manifest for the impoverished rural majority. Disillusionment spread, setting the stage for the 19th-century rise of Irish nationalism under leaders like Daniel O'Connell. Still, the constitutional transformation was now set: Ireland was bound to Great Britain under a single legislature, forging a new political entity that would endure—albeit contentiously—until the early 20th century.

15.6 Integration and Tensions Across the United Kingdom

By 1801, then, the islands off the northwestern coast of Europe were united—on paper—under one crown and one parliament, forming the United Kingdom of Great Britain and Ireland. In practice, regional identities and disparities remained strong:

- **Scotland** was by now thoroughly knitted into Britain's commercial and imperial projects, albeit with continuing economic hardship in parts of the Highlands.

- **Wales** was experiencing the beginnings of industrial expansion, especially in the south, even as the Welsh language persisted in religious and cultural life.
- **Ireland** entered the union under duress, with profound sectarian and economic divides still unresolved.

The next stage would see the UK enter a new century of European conflict with revolutionary and Napoleonic France. War, empire, and industrial transformation would shape the destiny of all four nations within the kingdom, sometimes uniting them in common cause, at other times exposing raw historical wounds. The close of this chapter brings us to the threshold of that era: 1801, the formal birth of the United Kingdom of Great Britain and Ireland, just as Napoleon rose to power across the Channel.

15.7 Summary of Chapter 15

Between 1783 and 1801, the relationships between England (or Britain) and its constituent nations—Scotland, Wales, and Ireland—underwent key developments:

1. **Scotland** continued its post-Jacobite transformation, with the Highland Clearances reshaping Gaelic culture and the Lowlands prospering through the Enlightenment and commerce.
2. **Wales** integrated further into the British state, with the first stirrings of industrial growth in coal and iron, while retaining a strong Welsh-language religious and cultural identity.
3. **Ireland** emerged as the most contentious part of the archipelago, experiencing sectarian divides, radical reform movements, and ultimately the 1798 Rebellion. British authorities concluded that only a formal union would stabilize Ireland.
4. **Acts of Union 1800** created the United Kingdom of Great Britain and Ireland, abolishing the Irish Parliament but failing initially to emancipate Ireland's Catholic majority, planting seeds for future unrest.

With the dawn of the 19th century, Britain stood at the brink of a massive conflict with Napoleon's France—an epochal struggle that would test its military, economic, and political fabric. This conflict and its aftermath form the focal point of the next chapter, as the newly constituted United Kingdom confronted both an external foe and internal challenges in an era of global war.

Chapter 16: The Napoleonic Wars and Their Effects on Britain (1801–1815)

Introduction
By 1801, the United Kingdom of Great Britain and Ireland had officially come into existence. That same year, across the English Channel, Napoleon Bonaparte held power in France, soon to proclaim himself Emperor (1804). The next 14 years would be consumed by a series of wars—collectively remembered as the Napoleonic Wars—pitting Britain and its allies against Napoleonic France. These wars were fought on multiple continents, from the Iberian Peninsula to the Middle East and beyond. For Britain, which relied on naval power and a potent alliance system, the stakes were existential: defeat could mean invasion, the collapse of empire, and the end of British influence in Europe.

This chapter will examine how the United Kingdom mobilized its military, economy, and society during the Napoleonic Wars, highlighting key battles, domestic reforms, and the war's lasting impact on British society. We will also track the contributions of figures like William Pitt the Younger, Horatio Nelson, and Arthur Wellesley (the future Duke of Wellington). By the war's end in 1815, Britain emerged with a stronger sense of national identity, a far-flung empire, and economic power—but also with significant social stresses that would erupt later in the century.

16.1 The Strategic Context of War

Britain's Naval Tradition
Long before Napoleon's rise, Britain had relied on its navy to project power and defend its island from invasion. This tradition became even more crucial once France dominated much of continental Europe. Britain's "wooden walls"—its ships of the line—guarded the Channel, patrolled the Atlantic, and harassed French commerce worldwide.

The Coalition System
Britain alone could not engage the full might of Napoleonic France on land. Hence, it financed and supported various coalitions with other European

powers—Austria, Russia, Prussia, Portugal, and later Spain. While these alliances often formed and dissolved quickly, Britain's gold (the so-called "Pitt's gold," referring to Prime Minister William Pitt the Younger) funded much of the continental resistance to France.

Potential Invasion
Napoleon toyed with plans to invade Britain, amassing troops along the Channel coast at Boulogne. The possibility of a French landing kept British public nerves on edge. Volunteer militias sprang up, and coastal fortifications were strengthened. Yet, as events would show, Napoleon's inability to secure maritime superiority proved decisive. Once French naval power was broken, Britain would remain unconquered.

16.2 Key Political Leadership

William Pitt the Younger
Pitt returned to office (in various spells) as prime minister at crucial moments. He had guided Britain through earlier conflicts with Revolutionary France. His policies included the suspension of certain civil liberties (e.g., the Habeas Corpus Suspension Act) to crack down on radical sympathies, a reflection of government paranoia that revolutionary ideals might spread. Pitt also managed the national finances, introducing new taxes and government bonds to finance the war effort.

Charles Fox and Political Divisions
Even amidst the war, domestic politics remained combative. The Whig opposition, led by Charles James Fox, often criticized the government's repressive measures and campaigned for peace negotiations. Some Whigs sympathized with aspects of French revolutionary principles, though Napoleon's authoritarian turn dampened that sympathy. The Napoleonic conflict polarized British politics, with some more radical voices suppressed under government suspicion.

Lord Liverpool and Later Leadership
After Pitt's death in 1806, several short ministries followed, culminating in Lord Liverpool becoming prime minister in 1812. Under Liverpool's steady, if cautious, leadership, Britain stayed the course of war until Napoleon's ultimate defeat. Liverpool then presided over the immediate post-war period, facing economic dislocation and demands for political reform.

16.3 The Naval War and Admiral Horatio Nelson

Trafalgar (1805)
Arguably the most famous naval engagement of the Napoleonic Wars, the Battle of Trafalgar saw Admiral Horatio Nelson's fleet defeat the combined Franco-Spanish navy off the coast of Spain. Nelson's bold tactics—sailing his columns directly into the enemy line—led to a decisive victory, though he was mortally wounded in the battle. Trafalgar ended any serious prospect of a French invasion, ensuring British naval dominance for the duration of the wars.

Nelson's Legacy
Nelson became a national hero, emblematic of courage and strategic genius. Public mourning followed his death, culminating in a state funeral. His column in London's Trafalgar Square (constructed later in the 19th century) would memorialize his achievements for generations. The Royal Navy, buoyed by this victory, focused thereafter on blockading French ports, strangling Napoleonic trade and limiting French colonial outreach.

16.4 The War on Land – Peninsular Campaign and Wellington

The Iberian Peninsula
The so-called Peninsular War (1808–1814) arose when Napoleon deposed the Spanish Bourbon monarchy and placed his brother Joseph on the Spanish throne, triggering widespread revolt. Britain backed the Spanish guerrillas and Portuguese allies. Arthur Wellesley landed in Portugal in 1808, leading British-Portuguese armies in a grueling campaign that eventually expelled French forces from the peninsula.

Guerrilla Warfare
The Spanish populace waged a vicious guerrilla war, attacking French supply lines and garrisons. The French, unaccustomed to such decentralized resistance, found themselves bogged down. British support, combined with Spanish and Portuguese resistance, forced the French into a protracted struggle, draining Napoleon's resources. Wellesley's victory at Vitoria (1813) helped dismantle French control in Spain, paving the way for an Allied march into southern France.

Rise of Wellington

Wellesley gained the title Duke of Wellington in recognition of his successes. His disciplined approach to logistics, training, and defensive tactics (famously using the "reverse slope" method to shield troops from artillery) won admiration. By the time Napoleon faced a multi-front war in 1813–1814, Wellington had secured the southwestern theatre of operations, contributing significantly to Napoleon's abdication in 1814.

16.5 The Home Front: Economy, Society, and Early Reform

Wartime Economy

Financing the Napoleonic Wars required unprecedented government borrowing. The national debt soared, but Britain's expanding commercial and industrial base—plus the stable currency managed by the Bank of England—allowed it to sustain the financial burden. Taxes increased, including the introduction of an income tax in 1799 (temporarily), which was reintroduced later. Blockades and continental warfare disrupted trade, but Britain's naval supremacy kept many maritime routes open.

Industrial Growth

Despite the disruptions of war, the early 19th century saw accelerating industrial development. Inventors perfected textile machinery; canals and roads improved internal transport. Factories expanded in Lancashire, the Midlands, and parts of Scotland. Urbanization proceeded rapidly, though living conditions in growing industrial cities were harsh. Child labor, long hours, and slum housing became more prevalent.

Social Unrest and Luddite Riots

New machinery threatened the livelihood of skilled artisans—particularly weavers and frame-knitters—leading to outbreaks of violence known as the Luddite riots (1811–1816). In Nottinghamshire, Yorkshire, and Lancashire, groups of workers smashed factory machines in protest. The government responded harshly, regarding such actions as seditious at a time of national emergency.

Political Dissent

The war atmosphere fed official suspicion of radical politics. Societies promoting parliamentary reform or discussing revolutionary ideas were closely monitored. Nonetheless, calls for reform persisted. Writers like William Cobbett criticized corruption and the lack of representation for industrial towns. Growing segments of the middle class—beneficiaries of commercial wealth—began to question the aristocratic monopoly on Parliament.

16.6 The Continental System and Britain's Trade

Napoleon's Continental System
In an attempt to cripple Britain economically, Napoleon declared the Continental System, barring British goods from ports under French control and pressuring neutral countries to comply. Britain retaliated with its own Orders in Council, imposing maritime restrictions on neutral shipping that traded with France. This economic warfare escalated tensions globally.

Global Trade Network
While the Continental System inflicted pain on British exports to Europe, Britain responded by expanding trade outside the continent—developing markets in Latin America, for instance, where revolutions against Spanish rule opened new opportunities for British merchants. The Royal Navy's blockade of Europe hampered French commerce as well, leading many in occupied countries to resent Napoleon's restrictions.

Impact on Neutral Powers
Countries like the United States found themselves caught between French decrees and British blockades, leading to the War of 1812 between Britain and the US. Although overshadowed by the broader Napoleonic conflict, this Anglo-American clash drained some British resources, requiring naval deployments to North America. Ultimately, the War of 1812 ended with no major territorial changes, but it tested Britain's capacity to fight on multiple fronts.

16.7 The Downfall of Napoleon and the Congress of Vienna

From Russia to Leipzig
Napoleon's ill-fated invasion of Russia in 1812, ending in a catastrophic retreat from Moscow, severely weakened French forces. The following year, the Sixth Coalition (Russia, Austria, Prussia, Britain, Sweden, and others) defeated Napoleon at Leipzig (the Battle of Nations). Wellington advanced from the south, pushing into southern France. By early 1814, Paris fell, and Napoleon abdicated, exiled to Elba.

The Hundred Days and Waterloo

Napoleon escaped Elba in 1815, rallied French troops, and attempted a final campaign. Britain and its allies mobilized swiftly. The climactic Battle of Waterloo (June 1815) in present-day Belgium saw Wellington's Anglo-Dutch-German forces, combined with the Prussians under Blücher, decisively defeat Napoleon. Exiled again, this time to Saint Helena, Napoleon never returned. The Napoleonic Wars were over.

Congress of Vienna (1814–1815)

Throughout 1814–1815, European diplomats met in Vienna to redraw the map of Europe. Britain's main goal was to ensure a stable balance of power that would prevent any single continental power from dominating again. While Britain did not seek large annexations in Europe, it secured or confirmed various colonial possessions gained during the wars (such as Cape Colony in South Africa). The result was a new order designed to maintain peace—though, as history would show, tensions would remain just beneath the surface.

16.8 War's Effects on British Society and Politics

Economic Aftermath

Victory left Britain as the world's leading naval and colonial power. However, the abrupt transition to peace in 1815 brought economic dislocations—demobilized soldiers and sailors flooded the labor market, causing unemployment. Wartime industries scaled down. Agricultural prices fell, prompting the government to pass the Corn Laws (1815), designed to protect domestic grain producers but criticized by many as harmful to consumers.

Social Tensions

The post-war slump led to widespread distress, especially among the working poor. In addition, the cost of living had risen during the war, while wages often lagged. This discontent fueled protests and calls for parliamentary reform. The government, fearful of a repeat of French revolutionary chaos, maintained strict policies, culminating in the Peterloo Massacre (1819)—a clash between cavalry and reform protesters in Manchester.

Fading of the Old Order?

Although the aristocracy remained powerful, cracks in the old social and political order were becoming visible. Industrialists in the new manufacturing cities demanded representation in Parliament. The spread of literacy, newspapers, and radical pamphlets ensured that political ideas reached broader segments of the population. While the major parliamentary reform acts would come later (notably in 1832), the Napoleonic era set the stage for these future transformations.

16.9 Military and Cultural Legacy

Army Reforms
During the wars, the British Army learned to coordinate large-scale campaigns in Europe, forging a proud military tradition that would echo into the Victorian age. The regimental system and the figure of the "Redcoat" soldier became iconic, though discipline was severe and conditions often harsh.

National Identity
Victories, particularly at Trafalgar and Waterloo, generated a surge of patriotic sentiment. Public ceremonies, monuments, and popular prints celebrated heroic leaders, from Nelson to Wellington. At the same time, the war drew the four nations of the newly created United Kingdom into a shared enterprise, reinforcing the sense (though never entirely uniform) of a collective British identity.

Literature and Arts
Artists and writers of the Romantic era, including William Wordsworth, Lord Byron, and J.M.W. Turner, were shaped by the Napoleonic conflict. Themes of liberty, heroism, nature, and the individual's struggle against tyranny permeated poetry, paintings, and essays. Turner's seascapes often captured the drama of naval engagements or storm-lashed vessels, reflecting the maritime soul of Britain.

16.10 Summary of Chapter 16

From 1801 to 1815, the newly formed United Kingdom of Great Britain and Ireland fought a titanic struggle against Napoleonic France. Key points include:

- **Naval Supremacy**: The Royal Navy's triumph at Trafalgar eliminated the risk of invasion and allowed Britain to blockade French ports.

- **Coalitions and Wellington**: Britain financed and supported continental allies, while Wellington's campaigns in the Iberian Peninsula and at Waterloo proved decisive on land.
- **Domestic Impacts**: Wartime borrowing, industrial expansion, and social strains shaped British society. Government repression of dissent was common, but demands for reform persisted.
- **Final Victory**: Napoleon's defeat and exile in 1815 ushered in a new European order, with Britain as a paramount maritime and imperial force. Post-war economic troubles and social tensions pointed toward upcoming shifts in the political landscape.

With the wars ended, Britain stood at a crossroads: triumphant abroad, yet confronted with significant challenges at home. As the 19th century advanced, industrialization accelerated, social reform movements gathered momentum, and the United Kingdom navigated the complexities of a rapidly changing world. The next chapters will delve into these transformations, continuing our journey through British history prior to the fully modern era.

Chapter 17: The Early 19th Century – Reform Movements and Industry (1815–1850)

Introduction
By 1815, Britain stood triumphant after the Napoleonic Wars. However, victory brought fresh challenges: widespread economic disruption, unemployment among demobilized soldiers, and social tensions stoked by rising industrialization. Over the following decades, the country would undergo dramatic changes. The Industrial Revolution—already underway—accelerated and reshaped work, living conditions, and national wealth. Meanwhile, a succession of reform campaigns pressed for changes in voting rights, workers' conditions, religious freedoms, and more. Although far from today's notion of democracy, Britain in the early 19th century took important steps toward greater political participation for many citizens.

This chapter surveys the major developments from the end of the Napoleonic Wars to approximately 1850, charting economic transformations, social unrest, and pivotal parliamentary reforms such as the Great Reform Act of 1832. We also examine key figures—reformers, industrialists, and statesmen—who propelled or resisted change. These four decades laid much of the groundwork for the Victorian era to come, with new technologies, middle-class influence, and expanding global power shaping Britain's outlook and identity.

17.1 Post-War Challenges and Social Unrest

Economic Dislocation After 1815
The sudden cessation of conflict with France disrupted wartime industries—shipyards, ordnance factories, and cavalry suppliers found demand evaporated. Soldiers and sailors were discharged in large numbers, crowding an already challenging labor market. War financing had driven up national debt, and while Britain's financial system was robust relative to continental powers, high taxes and government retrenchment followed.

Corn Laws and Political Backlash
Among the earliest contentious laws of the post-war years were the Corn Laws (reintroduced or tightened in 1815), designed to protect British grain producers

from cheaper foreign imports. When the price of grain (and thus bread) rose, the poor and the expanding urban population suffered. Public anger grew, especially in industrializing regions that relied on affordable food for their workforce. The Corn Laws became symbolic of aristocratic power protecting landowners' interests at the expense of the urban poor and industrial classes.

Unrest and Repression
In the years following Waterloo, popular discontent erupted in protests and sporadic violence. The government, fearful of revolutionary contagion from continental Europe, responded with harsh measures:

- **Spa Fields Riots (1816)** and **the March of the Blanketeers (1817)** showcased desperation among unemployed workers and radical reformers.
- **Suspension of Habeas Corpus** and passage of the **Seditious Meetings Acts** allowed authorities to detain suspected agitators without trial and restrict public gatherings.
- The **Peterloo Massacre (1819)** in Manchester, where cavalry charged a peaceful crowd demanding parliamentary reform, shocked the nation and became a rallying cry for reform movements.

Despite these crackdowns, calls for systemic change—in representation, workers' rights, and religious equality—did not dissipate. The stage was set for a major clash between reformers and the entrenched political establishment.

17.2 Industrial Expansion and Its Impact

Mechanization of Industry
By the early 19th century, Britain had moved beyond the pioneering stages of textile innovation into broader sectors. Key developments included:

- **Cotton and Textiles**: Spinning jennies, water frames, and power looms proliferated across Lancashire and the Midlands, driving down production costs and boosting exports.
- **Coal and Iron**: Mines in northern England, South Wales, and the Scottish Lowlands expanded rapidly to fuel steam engines and iron foundries. The "puddling and rolling" process improved iron quality, fueling a surge in metal goods and machinery.

- **Steam Power**: James Watt's refinements to the steam engine (patented decades earlier) found increasing application in factories, pumping systems, and later in locomotives.

Transport Revolution

Efficient transport was crucial to industrial success:

1. **Canals**: In the late 18th century, a canal-building frenzy had linked industrial regions with ports. By the 1810s and 1820s, canals transported bulk goods—coal, iron, finished textiles—at lower costs, although the canal era soon faced competition from railways.
2. **Turnpike Roads**: Private companies maintained improved roads and charged tolls. Stagecoaches carried passengers, while horse-drawn wagons hauled freight. Though an improvement over medieval tracks, roads could not match the capacity of water or rail transport.
3. **Railways**: The biggest leap came in the 1820s and 1830s with the development of steam locomotives. George Stephenson's **Stockton and Darlington Railway** (1825) and the **Liverpool and Manchester Railway** (1830) demonstrated rail's superior speed and reliability. The "railway mania" of the 1840s saw rapid expansion of lines connecting major cities, revolutionizing travel and distribution.

Urban Growth and Living Conditions

Factories clustered around coalfields or near ports, leading to the explosive growth of towns like Manchester, Birmingham, Leeds, and Glasgow. Housing for workers was hastily built:

- **Overcrowding**: Multiple families might share cramped rooms in cheaply erected tenements.
- **Sanitation Issues**: Open sewers, lack of clean water, and poor waste disposal led to frequent outbreaks of cholera and other diseases.
- **Working-Class Communities**: Despite dire conditions, new social networks emerged—friendly societies, chapels, and trade unions (albeit limited by law) provided mutual aid and a sense of identity.

Such conditions fueled calls for reform, from both philanthropic middle-class reformers appalled at urban squalor and from labor activists seeking better wages and hours.

17.3 The Push for Political Reform

Rotten Boroughs and an Unrepresentative System
Prior to 1832, Britain's parliamentary representation was notoriously skewed:

- **Boroughs** with very few inhabitants (sometimes only a handful of voters) still elected two MPs—so-called "rotten" or "pocket" boroughs easily controlled by local magnates.
- **Industrial Cities** like Manchester, Birmingham, and Leeds had no direct representation despite massive populations.
- Property qualifications restricted the franchise to a small minority of male property owners, leaving the majority voiceless.

This archaic system increasingly drew criticism, particularly as industrial areas grew in economic significance. Middle-class manufacturers, merchants, and professionals resented the dominance of landed aristocrats. Working-class radicals wanted universal suffrage, though that remained out of reach for the time being.

The Reform Act of 1832
After years of agitation, the Whig government under Earl Grey passed the **Reform Act (Great Reform Act) of 1832**, effecting significant—though limited—changes:

- **Redistribution of Seats**: Dozens of rotten boroughs were abolished or reduced in representation, with seats reallocated to rapidly growing industrial towns.
- **Expanded Electorate**: Property requirements were lowered so that more middle-class men could vote, roughly doubling the electorate (from about 5% to 10% of adult males).
- **Preservation of Aristocratic Influence**: Voting was still not secret (open ballots persisted until 1872), and the Act did not enfranchise the working class. Many radical reformers felt the changes insufficient.

Nevertheless, the 1832 Act was a watershed: it signaled Parliament's willingness to adapt to industrial realities and set a precedent for further electoral reforms.

Municipal and Other Reforms
Parliament also tackled local governance. The **Municipal Corporations Act (1835)** cleaned up corrupt town corporations, introducing elected councils in boroughs and standardizing administration. This shift empowered urban reformers to

address local issues like sanitation and policing. Meanwhile, philanthropic MPs sought legislative remedies for social ills, such as child labor in factories.

17.4 Social Legislation and Humanitarian Campaigns

Factory Acts

Growing public awareness of the harsh conditions in factories—especially for women and children—spurred early attempts at regulation:

- **Factory Act of 1833**: Limited the hours children could work in textile mills (no children under nine; ages 9–13 limited to 48 hours per week). It established inspectors to enforce compliance, though they were too few to be fully effective.
- **Mines and Collieries Act (1842)**: Prohibited women and girls, and boys under ten, from working underground. Though paternalistic by modern standards, it was a milestone in acknowledging that certain working conditions were too dangerous or morally objectionable.

Slavery Abolition

Britain's role in the transatlantic slave trade had long been a source of controversy. The **Slave Trade Act (1807)** ended the trade, but not slavery itself. The **Slavery Abolition Act (1833)**, spearheaded by figures like William Wilberforce and Thomas Clarkson, finally abolished slavery in most British colonies, with some transitional "apprenticeships" continuing until 1838. While these reforms did not end global slavery, they marked a major moral victory for British abolitionists.

Religious Toleration

Though still an Anglican-dominated society, the early 19th century saw a gradual easing of restrictions:

- **Catholic Emancipation Act (1829)**: Ended most of the legal barriers preventing Catholics from serving in Parliament and certain public offices, though suspicion of Catholicism remained widespread.
- **Repeal of Test and Corporation Acts (1828)**: Removed the requirement that officials in corporations or government be communicant members of the Church of England, thus aiding Protestant dissenters.

Such legislation signaled the slow erosion of confessional barriers, though prejudice and legal inequalities did not vanish overnight.

17.5 Chartism and the Working-Class Movement

Origins of Chartism

Even after the 1832 Reform Act, the working class found themselves disenfranchised. Economic downturns, wage cuts, and poor living conditions fueled discontent. In 1838, radical leaders drafted the **People's Charter**, demanding:

1. Universal male suffrage
2. Secret ballot
3. Equal electoral districts
4. No property qualifications for MPs
5. Payment for MPs (allowing working men to serve)
6. Annual general elections

This platform, known as Chartism, attracted mass support from factory workers, artisans, and some middle-class radicals who felt that the limited 1832 reforms had not gone far enough.

Petitions and Unrest

Chartists organized large-scale meetings, marches, and petition drives. In 1839, 1842, and 1848, they submitted massive petitions to Parliament—each signed by millions of supporters. Parliament repeatedly dismissed these petitions, provoking anger. Some Chartists urged peaceful lobbying, while others flirted with violence, resulting in confrontations like the **Newport Rising (1839)** in South Wales. Repression followed, with arrests and imprisonment for leading activists.

Long-Term Legacy

Though the Chartist movement fragmented by the late 1840s, many of its core demands would eventually be adopted (though not annual elections). Universal male suffrage, the secret ballot, and payment of MPs all became law in subsequent decades. The Chartists thus served as a bridge between early 19th-century radicalism and later labor and social-democratic movements.

17.6 Middle-Class Influence and the Repeal of the Corn Laws

Rise of the Middle Class
Industrial prosperity created a substantial middle class: factory owners, merchants, bankers, and professionals. They campaigned for government policies favoring free trade, minimal regulation of industry (beyond certain social reforms), and the moral virtues of self-help and responsibility. Politically, many middle-class men gained the vote under the 1832 Act, forming a liberal bloc that challenged traditional landed aristocratic power.

Anti-Corn Law League
One of the most successful middle-class campaigns was the **Anti-Corn Law League**, founded in 1838 by Richard Cobden, John Bright, and others. They argued that high food prices hurt workers' purchasing power and stifled industrial growth. Through pamphlets, lectures, and mass meetings, the League built nationwide support:

- **Free Trade Advocacy**: The League insisted that removing tariffs on grain imports would foster competition, reduce bread prices, and encourage reciprocal trade agreements with other countries.
- **Moral and Humanitarian Rhetoric**: They denounced the Corn Laws as an example of aristocratic selfishness, blaming them for exacerbating poverty among the urban poor.

Repeal (1846)
Despite resistance from rural Tory MPs, Prime Minister Sir Robert Peel, a Conservative who recognized the economic logic of free trade, pushed through the repeal of the Corn Laws in 1846 (ironically splitting his party). This momentous victory for liberal, industrial interests indicated how much political influence had shifted toward the urban middle class. Peel's personal sacrifice—he resigned soon after—underscored how divisive the issue had been. Nevertheless, free trade became a hallmark of British economic policy into the mid-Victorian period.

17.7 Cultural Currents and Intellectual Debate

Romanticism and Reaction
The Romantic movement, which had arisen during the Napoleonic era, continued to flourish. Poets like Lord Byron, Percy Bysshe Shelley, and John

Keats produced works emphasizing emotion, nature, and individualism—often critiquing industrialization's dehumanizing aspects. Some turned their attention to contemporary issues like oppression in Greece (Byron) or the plight of the working class (Shelley's radical stances). Prose writers, including essayists like Charles Lamb and Thomas De Quincey, explored introspection and personal experience.

Utilitarianism
Intellectuals such as Jeremy Bentham and, later, John Stuart Mill championed **utilitarianism**, the idea that policies should promote "the greatest happiness of the greatest number." This philosophy influenced debates about legal reform, prison conditions, and the extension of the franchise. Bentham's push for rational law codes and institutions resonated with reform-minded MPs seeking to modernize Britain's archaic legal framework. Mill, in particular, added concerns about individual liberty and moral progress, foreshadowing arguments for broader democratic rights, women's emancipation, and social welfare.

Religious and Philosophical Ferment
The established Church of England saw challenges from multiple fronts. The Oxford Movement (1830s–1840s) emphasized a return to older Catholic-like rituals within Anglicanism, sparking controversy about church identity. Dissenting chapels thrived among both middle-class Liberals and working-class radicals, forging strong local communities. Religious debates intersected with social questions—Should Christians support paternalistic charity or champion structural reform? Should Sunday schools and missionary societies cater to the poor at home or abroad?

17.8 The Great Famine in Ireland and Its Influence

Tragedy in Ireland
Though the Act of Union (1801) tied Ireland to Britain, governance largely neglected pressing social problems. When potato blight struck in 1845, destroying the staple crop that fed millions of Irish peasantry, famine ensued. Over the next several years, starvation and disease ravaged the population, leading to an estimated one million deaths and a wave of emigration (mainly to North America).

Government Response
Prime Minister Sir Robert Peel initially authorized some relief measures,

including importing Indian corn (nicknamed "Peel's Brimstone") from the U.S. But subsequent governments—particularly that of Lord John Russell—adhered to a laissez-faire philosophy, limiting direct intervention. Workhouses became overwhelmed, and public works projects proved insufficient. The crisis revealed the inadequacy of existing social structures and the deep inequities in land ownership. Irish anger and distrust of British rule intensified.

Long-Term Consequences
The famine underscored the moral and political questions swirling around the role of the state. Critics accused the government of genocide or at least negligence. Irish emigration soared, reshaping the demographics of Britain and overseas dominions. Calls for Irish self-governance (Home Rule) would gain momentum in the later 19th century. Meanwhile, the tragedy further eroded belief in purely market-based solutions to humanitarian crises, though it would take decades for more robust social interventions to emerge.

17.9 Entering the Mid-Victorian Era

By 1850, Britain had navigated numerous upheavals. The monarchy, under King George IV (until 1830) and then William IV (1830–1837), had remained influential, though not omnipotent. Queen Victoria's accession in 1837 ushered in a new age of stable, relatively popular monarchy. Politically, the aristocratic grip on power was slowly yielding to the influence of an ascendant middle class. Industrialization continued apace, heralding both national prosperity (for some) and profound social challenges.

In summary, from 1815 to 1850, the nation endured deep rifts—between landed interests and industrial capital, between privileged elites and disenfranchised masses, between defenders of old ways and champions of progress. While not all demands for change were met, major steps—most notably the Reform Act of 1832 and the repeal of the Corn Laws—signaled the capacity of Britain's political system to reform itself incrementally rather than succumbing to outright revolution, as seen elsewhere in Europe. These decades laid the foundations of the Victorian order, which would soon face fresh tests of empire, competition, and internal social reform.

17.10 Summary of Chapter 17

From the aftermath of the Napoleonic Wars in 1815 to the midpoint of the 19th century, Britain experienced:

- **Economic and Industrial Growth**: Rapid factory expansion, transport revolutions (canals, then railways), and urbanization.
- **Social Tensions and Reform**: Popular unrest over the Corn Laws, labor conditions, and unrepresentative politics. The Great Reform Act (1832) and early Factory Acts exemplified gradual but significant legislative changes.
- **Rising Middle-Class Power**: Merchant and industrial elites increasingly shaped political discourse, culminating in the repeal of the Corn Laws (1846).
- **Radical Movements**: Chartism demanded universal male suffrage and other democratic measures, foreshadowing future reforms.
- **Cultural and Intellectual Vibrancy**: Romanticism, utilitarianism, and religious debates influenced social attitudes.
- **Irish Crisis**: The Great Famine (1845–1849) exposed the limits of laissez-faire governance and deepened Irish grievances against British rule.

Poised on the brink of the Victorian era, Britain in 1850 had become the leading industrial power, its empire beginning to expand more aggressively. The stage was set for the next half-century of transformation, as the country navigated unprecedented technological progress, colonial ambitions, and the moral dilemmas posed by stark social inequalities.

Chapter 18: Mid to Late 19th Century – Victorian Transformations (1850–1901)

Introduction
The span from 1850 to 1901, dominated by the reign of Queen Victoria (r. 1837–1901), marks one of the most iconic periods in British history. During these decades, Britain experienced explosive industrial growth, imperial expansion, key social reforms, and vast cultural achievements—dubbed the "Victorian Age." This era's complexities ran deeper than its glossy self-image: behind displays of bourgeois respectability lay persistent social problems, debates over governance, and tensions stirred by scientific, religious, and economic change.

In this chapter, we examine the core transformations of the mid to late Victorian period. We explore major parliamentary reforms that broadened suffrage, the rapid acceleration of industrial and urban development, and the consolidation of an empire that spanned the globe. Key figures—Prime Ministers like Lord Palmerston, William Ewart Gladstone, Benjamin Disraeli, and later Lord Salisbury—shaped domestic and foreign policy. Amid these shifts, Victorian society grappled with the meaning of progress, the responsibilities of empire, and the moral imperatives of religion and social conscience.

18.1 The Great Exhibition and the Triumph of Industry

Crystal Palace and Symbolic Display
A defining moment of the early Victorian era was the **Great Exhibition of the Works of Industry of All Nations** (1851), held in London's Hyde Park. Housed in the purpose-built Crystal Palace—an architectural marvel of glass and iron—this exhibition showcased British manufacturing prowess and hosted international exhibits:

- **Symbol of Modernity**: Over six million visitors attended, admiring machinery, textiles, and exotic displays from around the world. The event championed free trade and peaceful competition among nations.

- **National Pride and Optimism**: To Victorians, the Exhibition embodied the possibilities of human ingenuity and industrial progress. It also reinforced Britain's self-perception as a global leader in technology and commerce.

Railway Mania and Urban Development

By the 1850s, the railway network crisscrossed Britain, linking major cities and ports. This spurred suburban growth, allowed faster movement of goods, and further integrated the domestic market:

- **Economic Integration**: Regions specialized in particular industries—Lancashire for cotton, Yorkshire for wool, the Black Country for metalworks, and so on—knowing the railways could swiftly connect them to suppliers and customers.
- **City Expansion**: Populations in London, Manchester, Birmingham, and other urban centers skyrocketed. Metropolitan improvements, though slow and uneven, began to include sewage systems (pioneered by Joseph Bazalgette in London) and piped water.
- **Architectural Shifts**: Train stations like London's King's Cross or St Pancras epitomized Victorian engineering grandeur, while new civic buildings in industrial towns expressed local pride.

18.2 Political Leadership and Further Reform

Palmerston and Mid-Century Liberalism

Lord Palmerston (Henry John Temple) served as Foreign Secretary, then Prime Minister (1855–1858, 1859–1865). His tenure saw a robust foreign policy—intervening in European affairs to support liberal movements, balancing power in Europe, and ensuring Britain's trade interests. Domestically, Palmerston was more conservative, cautious about sweeping reform. His personal popularity, especially during conflicts like the Crimean War (1853–1856), secured him repeated electoral success.

Second Reform Act (1867)

Under the Conservative Prime Minister Benjamin Disraeli, responding to increasing public pressure, Parliament passed the **Reform Act of 1867**, which:

- Expanded the electorate further, granting the vote to many urban working-class men (though still excluding agricultural laborers and most unskilled workers).

- Nearly doubled the number of voters again, accelerating the shift in political power away from rural elites towards urban areas.
- Reinforced the notion that peaceful agitation could bring incremental reform, forestalling the kind of violent upheaval seen in some European states.

Gladstone vs. Disraeli Rivalry

The late 1860s and 1870s witnessed a famous rivalry between two towering statesmen:

1. **William Ewart Gladstone (Liberal)**: Advocated for freer trade, Irish disestablishment (the Irish Church Act, 1869), and further democratization. A moralist, Gladstone championed causes like civil service reform and sought to reduce public expenditures.
2. **Benjamin Disraeli (Conservative)**: Emphasized empire, social paternalism (passing public health laws and artisan dwellings acts), and the symbolism of monarchy. Under Disraeli, Queen Victoria was crowned Empress of India (1877), reflecting a new imperial flamboyance.

Both leaders jockeyed to claim the mantle of reform. Gladstone's **Education Act (1870)** advanced elementary education, while Disraeli's government introduced measures improving working-class housing and hygiene. This competition spurred an evolving acceptance that government should address social ills, albeit incrementally.

18.3 Social and Labor Conditions

Industrial Workforce

Factories and mines remained harsh environments for workers. Gradual improvements in safety, hours, and wages occurred, but these were hard-won:

- **Trade Unions**: Legal restrictions had eased after 1824–1825, though union activity was still closely policed. By the 1850s and 1860s, new model unions representing skilled workers emerged, bargaining for better conditions.
- **Strikes and Collective Action**: High-profile disputes, like the engineers' strikes of the late 1850s, illustrated growing worker confidence. Yet large segments of the labor force—women, unskilled laborers, agricultural workers—remained underrepresented.

Public Health and Urban Living

The mid-Victorian age gradually recognized the link between sanitation and health:

- **Public Health Acts (1848, 1872, 1875)** incrementally gave local authorities powers to regulate housing, sewers, and water supply, though enforcement varied widely.
- Philanthropists and reformers, including Octavia Hill, tackled slum housing, founding charitable trusts for model dwellings.
- Infectious diseases (cholera, typhus, smallpox) still posed major threats; vaccination acts and better waste disposal helped reduce mortality rates over time.

Education and Literacy

The Education Act of 1870 began the process of establishing board schools in areas where church or charitable schools were absent. By the 1880s, schooling for children aged 5–10 became compulsory, though not free until the 1890s. Literacy surged, fueling a rise in newspapers, periodicals, and novels—many consumed by an emerging literate working and middle class. Authors like Charles Dickens, Elizabeth Gaskell, and later Thomas Hardy explored social issues in their works, shaping public discourse on class and morality.

18.4 The Expanding British Empire

Imperial Ambitions and "Informal Empire"

Beyond the formal colonies (India, Canada, Australia, the Caribbean), Britain extended its economic and political influence in Latin America, the Middle East, and East Asia through trade concessions, naval power, and financial investments. This "informal empire" often allowed Britain to dominate local markets without direct governance.

India and the Raj

After the **Indian Rebellion (1857–1858)**, the British Crown took direct control of India from the East India Company, marking the start of the **British Raj** (from 1858). The Government of India Act (1858) appointed a Viceroy, overshadowing the old Company directors. Queen Victoria's title as Empress of India (1877) reflected Britain's heightened self-image as a global imperial power.

- **Infrastructure Projects**: Railways, canals, and telegraphs were built to facilitate trade and military movement.
- **Social and Cultural Impact**: Debates arose over how deeply Britain should intervene in Indian customs; some Victorian liberals championed "civilizing missions," while others recognized the complexities of local traditions.

Africa and Beyond

Though the "Scramble for Africa" is typically dated to the 1880s and 1890s, mid-century explorers like David Livingstone stirred public fascination with the continent. Britain's presence in coastal areas (e.g., Cape Colony, West African ports) laid foundations for later expansion. Meanwhile, disputes over trade in China (the Opium Wars, 1839–1842, 1856–1860) underscored the ruthlessness of Britain's mercantile pursuits. The resulting "treaty ports" system exemplified Victorian imperial arrogance.

18.5 Religion, Morality, and Victorian Values

The Evangelical Movement

Evangelical Christianity, influential since the late 18th century, thrived under Victorian morals. Key aspects included:

- **Personal Piety**: Emphasis on Bible reading, prayer, and moral living.
- **Social Activism**: Evangelicals championed missionary work abroad and philanthropic endeavors at home—campaigns against slavery, drunkenness (temperance societies), and prostitution.
- **Influence on Public Life**: Figures like Lord Shaftesbury, an evangelical aristocrat, pushed for factory and mine reforms, limiting child labor.

Respectability and Self-Help

Victorian society prized "respectability"—adherence to moral codes, industriousness, and family duty. Samuel Smiles's book **Self-Help (1859)** epitomized this ethos, claiming individual perseverance and virtue led to success. However, critics noted that poverty and exploitation often resulted from structural inequalities, not personal failings.

Challenges to Faith

The second half of the 19th century brought scientific and intellectual challenges to traditional Christianity:

- **Darwin's Theory of Evolution**: Charles Darwin's *On the Origin of Species* (1859) contested literal Biblical creation accounts, sparking fierce debate between scientists and theologians.
- **Higher Criticism**: Scholars examined Biblical texts with historical-critical methods, questioning authorship and historical accuracy.
- **Secularization and Doubt**: While many Victorians remained devout, a growing minority wrestled with skepticism. Literature (e.g., George Eliot's novels) portrayed characters facing crises of faith.

18.6 The Later Reform Acts and Democratic Evolution

The Ballot Act (1872)
One of the next big steps was the introduction of a **secret ballot**, reducing bribery and intimidation in elections. Public voting had led to widespread corruption; employers and landlords often coerced dependents to vote a certain way. With secret ballots, working-class voters could exercise greater independence, slowly leveling the political playing field.

Third Reform Act (1884–1885)
Continuing the path set by 1832 and 1867, Gladstone's government enacted further franchise expansions:

- **Enfranchisement of Agricultural Laborers**: The rural working class finally gained voting rights, bringing the electorate close to a majority of adult men.
- **Redrawing Electoral Boundaries**: The Redistribution of Seats Act (1885) eliminated many remaining inequalities, ensuring more equitable representation for populous areas.

Yet, universal male suffrage was still not complete—some men (domestic servants, for instance) were excluded, and women's suffrage was not yet on the mainstream political agenda. Nonetheless, the Victorian era ended with Britain significantly more democratic than at its start, albeit still short of modern standards.

18.7 Social Welfare and Emergent Labor Movements

Philanthropy and Early State Intervention
Religious societies, charitable trusts, and local councils offered limited relief for the destitute. The **Poor Law Amendment Act (1834)**—earlier in the century—had enforced harsh workhouse conditions, but by the late 19th century, more voices called for state-led improvements:

- **Public Health**: Subsequent Public Health Acts and local bylaws regulated sewage, slum clearance, and disease control.
- **Education Acts**: The 1870 and 1880 Acts expanded schooling, culminating in the 1891 decision to provide free elementary education in England and Wales.
- **Factory and Workshop Acts**: A series of further acts regulated women's and children's work hours and introduced safety standards.

Trade Union Growth
From the 1870s onward, **New Unionism** emerged, organizing unskilled laborers—dockers, gasworkers, matchgirls—rather than just skilled artisans. Strikes like the London Dock Strike (1889) demonstrated growing confidence among laborers. Socialist ideas, promoted by figures like Henry Hyndman (Social Democratic Federation) or William Morris, gained a foothold, although the mainstream labor movement remained moderate, seeking better wages and conditions rather than radical revolution.

18.8 Cultural Flourishing and Contradictions

Literature and the Novel
The Victorian era saw a golden age of the English novel, with authors capturing everyday life, social problems, and moral quandaries:

- **Charles Dickens**: Exposed urban poverty and child suffering in works like *Oliver Twist* and *Hard Times*.
- **Charlotte and Emily Brontë**: Explored female independence and gothic romance in *Jane Eyre* and *Wuthering Heights*.
- **Thomas Hardy**: Examined rural life's hardships, social conventions, and tragic fates in *Tess of the d'Urbervilles* and *Jude the Obscure* (the latter appeared just after the Victorian period but was strongly shaped by it).

Art and Aesthetic Movements

Victorian visual arts ranged from the sentimental moral paintings of the Royal Academy to the **Pre-Raphaelite Brotherhood**, which sought medieval-inspired detail and vivid color. Later in the century, the **Arts and Crafts Movement** (led by William Morris) reacted against industrial mass production, advocating handcraftsmanship and aesthetic beauty in everyday objects. The contradictory impulses of celebrating industrial progress versus yearning for romanticized pasts defined much Victorian cultural life.

Scientific Advance

The late Victorian period witnessed major strides in science and technology:

- **Medicine**: Louis Pasteur and Joseph Lister's work on germ theory and antiseptic surgery, while continental-based, profoundly affected British hospitals. Mortality rates in surgeries dropped.
- **Engineering Feats**: Isambard Kingdom Brunel's bridges, steamships (like the SS Great Eastern), and railway lines exemplified Victorian engineering ambition.
- **Communications**: The telegraph and, later, the telephone (Alexander Graham Bell, 1876) transformed global connectivity. Britain's imperial network benefited from undersea cables linking distant colonies.

18.9 The Approach to the 20th Century

Imperial Zenith and Challenges

By the 1890s, Britain controlled an empire "on which the sun never set," with territories in Africa, Asia, and the Pacific. Yet rival powers—Germany, the United States, and others—industrialized rapidly. Economic competition grew fiercer, and Britain began to question the security of its maritime dominance. Colonial conflicts—such as the Anglo-Zulu War (1879) or the Sudan campaigns (1880s-1890s)—prompted debates about the ethics and cost of expansion.

Social Reform and the Seeds of the Welfare State

Organizations like the **Fabian Society** (founded 1884) argued for gradual socialist reform. Investigations into poverty by Charles Booth in London and Seebohm Rowntree in York revealed shocking levels of deprivation, challenging the optimism that individual charity alone could suffice. The emergent **Independent Labour Party** (1893), led by figures like Keir Hardie, aimed to represent working-class interests in Parliament—a direct outgrowth of Victorian labor campaigns.

Women's Rights

Late Victorian feminists, including Josephine Butler (campaigning against the Contagious Diseases Acts) and Millicent Fawcett (promoting women's suffrage), began to coalesce into an organized movement. Although the vote remained elusive, property rights for married women improved (Married Women's Property Acts of 1870 and 1882). Educational opportunities also broadened; universities like London, Oxford, and Cambridge gradually opened degrees to women, though with many restrictions.

18.10 Summary of Chapter 18

Between 1850 and 1901, Britain underwent vast changes under the broad canopy of the Victorian era:

- **Industrial and Urban Growth**: Powered by railways, coal, and global trade, British industry reached unprecedented heights. Cities swelled, forging new social and cultural milieus.
- **Political Reforms**: The Second and Third Reform Acts (1867, 1884–85) expanded the electorate, while the secret ballot (1872) curbed electoral corruption. Prime ministers Disraeli and Gladstone championed different visions of empire, social policy, and constitutional development.
- **Social Legislation and Class Dynamics**: Factory acts, public health measures, and philanthropic endeavors gradually improved living conditions. However, class divides persisted, with the labor movement gaining momentum toward the century's end.
- **Cultural Achievements**: Literature, art, and science flourished, reflecting a society both enamored with progress and troubled by moral and religious dilemmas. The tension between industrial triumph and nostalgic idealism shaped Victorian self-identity.
- **Empire and International Competition**: Britain reached the apex of its imperial extent, but foreign rivals grew. Colonial wars and political debates about the morality of empire foreshadowed the 20th-century challenges.

By 1901, with the death of Queen Victoria, Britain stood at a turning point. The empire, though vast, faced emerging challenges at home and abroad. Rapid social change, the stirrings of new political ideologies (socialism, feminism), and the accelerating pace of global competition set the stage for the 20th century. The Victorian legacy—confidence in progress, complex moral standards, an evolving democracy—would profoundly influence the decades ahead, as Britain navigated two world wars, decolonization, and the modern age. Yet those developments lie beyond our current historical scope. For now, we conclude this chapter with the realization that the Victorian era's transformations laid much of the foundation for Britain's entry into modern times, even as unresolved questions lingered beneath its polished surface.

Chapter 19: The Dawn of the 20th Century – Imperial Height and Social Shifts (1901–1914)

Introduction
On January 22, 1901, Queen Victoria passed away after a reign of over sixty-three years. Her death symbolically closed the door on the 19th century that had borne her name. Yet the transitions shaping Britain were far more than symbolic. The first years of the 20th century—often referred to as the **Edwardian era** (1901–1910) under King Edward VII, followed by the early reign of George V—were defined by a mix of optimism and anxiety. The United Kingdom sat astride the globe with the largest empire in history, commanding trade routes, naval supremacy, and colonies on every continent. At home, however, the social fabric was being tested by rising demands for democracy, labor rights, and women's suffrage. Scientific and intellectual currents, along with new cultural forms, challenged traditional Victorian mores.

In this chapter, we will examine Britain at the apex of its imperial power and the social transformations that accompanied such power. We will see how politics began to shift, from aristocratic dominance to more populist energies, culminating in battles over welfare legislation, Irish Home Rule, and women's rights. By 1914, Britain's confidence would be tested by international rivalries, especially with a rising Germany, setting the stage for conflict that would disrupt the old world order.

19.1 The Edwardian Era and the Monarchy

Edward VII (1901–1910)
After Queen Victoria's death, her son Edward VII ascended the throne. Though already nearly sixty years old, Edward ushered in a lighter mood at court—less austere and more cosmopolitan than his mother's. Known for his sociability and personal charm, he traveled extensively in Europe, forging diplomatic ties. Edward's active role in foreign affairs (sometimes referred to as "the Uncle of Europe," given his familial links to many royal houses) influenced Britain's stance in the complex web of continental alliances.

George V (1910–1936)

Upon Edward's death in 1910, the crown passed to his son, George V. Though less flamboyant, George V was dedicated and dutiful. He would guide Britain through significant trials—most notably World War I—but in these prewar years, he largely deferred to the evolving structures of parliamentary government. The monarchy retained ceremonial prestige, commanding popular affection, but real power increasingly lay with elected representatives, especially as new social forces pushed for political reform.

Continuity and Change

Despite an outward appearance of continuity—rituals of state, aristocratic pomp, and empire's grandeur—the monarchy in the Edwardian period was adapting to a more media-driven age. Improved newspaper printing, photography, and the nascent film industry brought royal affairs closer to the public. Meanwhile, behind the scenes, social tensions percolated, from suffragettes confronting the royal establishment to labor unions challenging the status quo. The monarchy thus stood both as a symbol of tradition and a mediator in a changing political landscape.

19.2 The Empire at Its Zenith

Territorial Reach

By the early 1900s, the British Empire spanned territories in Africa (Egypt, Sudan, South Africa, Nigeria, Gold Coast, Kenya, etc.), Asia (the Indian subcontinent, Malaya, Hong Kong), the Caribbean, Canada, Australia, and New Zealand. Territorial acquisitions in Africa had surged during the "Scramble for Africa" of the 1880s–1890s. In many ways, Britain's self-identity was inseparable from its imperial role. The monarchy had become "Imperial," with Victoria crowned Empress of India in 1877 and subsequent monarchs adopting a global aura.

Imperial Administration

While the Crown retained ultimate sovereignty, actual governance involved a complex patchwork:

1. **Dominions** (Canada, Australia, New Zealand, and later South Africa) enjoyed substantial self-rule via their own parliaments but recognized the British monarch as head of state.

2. **Crown Colonies** were administered directly from London through appointed governors.
3. **Protectorates** or "informal empire" territories had local rulers under British "advice."

The India Office, Colonial Office, and Foreign Office juggled responsibilities, though coordination was challenging. Gradually, "nationhood" sentiments emerged in the Dominions, presaging future autonomy.

Public Attitudes Toward Empire
At home, a large section of the public celebrated empire. School curricula, popular literature, and events such as the 1897 Diamond Jubilee of Victoria or Edward VII's coronation in 1902 glorified Britain's "civilizing mission." Boy Scouts and Girl Guides movements—founded by Robert Baden-Powell—instilled imperial virtues of duty and service in youth. However, critics emerged, including socialists, pacifists, and some liberal intellectuals, who questioned the morality of subjugation and economic exploitation. Irish nationalists likewise viewed British imperial claims as hypocrisy while Ireland itself was denied self-governance.

Challenges Abroad
The empire was not unchallenged. Resistance flared periodically—uprisings in Africa, national movements in India, and economic competition from the United States and Germany. The **Anglo-Boer Wars** (the second of which ended in 1902) had already eroded Britain's self-assurance by revealing the harshness of colonial conflict, including the use of concentration camps for Boer civilians. Criticisms at home pressed for more humane imperial policies, though many Britons continued to see empire as a source of global stability and British prestige.

19.3 Domestic Politics: Liberals, Conservatives, and the Rise of Labour

Party Realignments
Edwardian politics featured two established parties—the **Conservatives (Tories)** and the **Liberals (Whigs historically, but now reformed into the modern Liberal Party)**—plus a growing **Labour** presence. The late Victorian era had ended with divisions in the Liberal Party over Irish Home Rule, but under Sir Henry Campbell-Bannerman and Herbert Henry Asquith, the Liberals regrouped, promoting social reforms and free trade. The Conservatives, though strong

under Lord Salisbury, faced leadership challenges after his retirement, eventually rallying behind Arthur Balfour and, somewhat later, Andrew Bonar Law.

The Labour Representation Committee and Emergence of Labour

A pivotal development was the founding of the **Labour Representation Committee (LRC) in 1900**, backed by trade unions and socialist societies like the Fabian Society. The LRC gained traction, securing parliamentary seats for Labour MPs who represented working-class interests more directly than the Liberals or Tories. By 1906, the LRC rebranded as the **Labour Party**, beginning a slow but steady climb that would eventually reshape British politics in the 20th century.

The Liberal Landslide of 1906

In the general election of 1906, the Liberals achieved a landslide victory, capitalizing on widespread dissatisfaction with the Boer War, Conservative education policies, and high tariffs proposed by Joseph Chamberlain. With a huge Commons majority, Liberal statesmen—Asquith, David Lloyd George, Winston Churchill (then a Liberal), and others—launched an ambitious program of social legislation, from pensions to health insurance. This heralded the first wave of what many dubbed the "Welfare State," although it remained limited in scope compared to later expansions.

19.4 Social Reforms and the Foundations of the Welfare State

The New Liberalism

From around 1906 to 1914, **"New Liberal"** ideas flourished. Unlike classical laissez-faire Liberalism, which stressed minimal state intervention, New Liberals recognized that the state might need to address poverty, health, and education to ensure true individual opportunity. Influential thinkers such as Leonard Trelawny Hobhouse and John A. Hobson argued that only an active government could correct market failures and social injustices.

Key Legislation

Several groundbreaking acts passed:

1. **Old Age Pensions Act (1908)**: Provided modest pensions for citizens over seventy of limited means.
2. **Trade Boards Act (1909)**: Set minimum wages in certain low-paid industries (like chain-making and lace).

3. **National Insurance Act (1911)**: Introduced health insurance for workers earning below a certain threshold, plus unemployment insurance in seasonal trades such as shipbuilding.
4. **Shops Act (1911)**: Regulated shop workers' hours, granting half-day closing.

While these reforms were modest by later standards, they represented a major shift from the Victorian Poor Law tradition. They also sparked fierce resistance from Conservatives, who saw high government spending and taxes as threatening property rights and Britain's economic competitiveness.

The People's Budget (1909)
Chancellor of the Exchequer **David Lloyd George** proposed the so-called "People's Budget" in 1909, aiming to fund new social programs through increased taxation on land and higher incomes. The House of Lords—dominated by Conservative aristocrats—vetoed the budget, igniting a constitutional crisis. Eventually, after two general elections in 1910 and the threat to flood the Lords with Liberal peers, the **Parliament Act of 1911** was passed. It curtailed the Lords' power to block money bills and reduced the maximum duration of a parliamentary term from seven years to five, thus affirming the dominance of the elected Commons over the hereditary chamber.

19.5 Women's Suffrage Movement

WSPU and Militant Campaigns
The Victorian era had left women largely disenfranchised. By the early 20th century, the suffrage movement gained momentum. The **Women's Social and Political Union (WSPU)**, founded in 1903 by Emmeline Pankhurst and her daughters Christabel and Sylvia, adopted militant tactics—disrupting political meetings, chaining themselves to railings, smashing windows—to force the issue of votes for women into the national spotlight. Their motto, "Deeds, not Words," reflected frustration at decades of polite lobbying that had yielded little change.

Peaceful Suffragists
Meanwhile, the non-militant wing—led by Millicent Fawcett's **National Union of Women's Suffrage Societies (NUWSS)**—employed constitutional methods, lobbying MPs, organizing peaceful demonstrations, and forging alliances with male supporters. Tensions sometimes ran high between the militant and

non-militant wings, yet both contributed to keeping women's suffrage in public debate.

Government Response
Suffragettes were frequently arrested. In prison, many conducted hunger strikes, leading authorities to forcibly feed them—a practice widely condemned as brutal. The government remained divided; some Liberals, like Winston Churchill, were reluctant to enfranchise women under perceived threats of militancy. By 1914, partial suffrage for women had garnered increasing parliamentary support, but progress stalled as a more dire international crisis loomed. Ultimately, limited women's suffrage would be granted in 1918, after World War I, and full equality in 1928—but these changes were rooted in the Edwardian struggle.

19.6 Ireland: Home Rule and Rising Tensions

The Irish Question
Ireland remained a thorny issue in British politics. Prime Minister Gladstone had attempted Irish Home Rule bills in 1886 and 1893, both defeated. By the early 1900s, with the Liberals again in power, the demand for an **Irish Parliament** to manage domestic affairs grew more urgent. **John Redmond** led the Irish Parliamentary Party in Westminster, pushing for a renewed Home Rule bill.

Unionist Resistance
Irish **Unionists**, particularly in Ulster (Protestant-majority northern counties), vehemently opposed Home Rule, fearing it would place them under a Catholic-dominated Dublin government. They formed paramilitary organizations, such as the **Ulster Volunteers (1912)**, pledging to resist by force if necessary. Meanwhile, southern Irish nationalists mobilized the **Irish Volunteers** in response. Political compromise proved elusive.

Third Home Rule Bill (1912)
The Liberal government introduced a third Home Rule Bill in 1912, which passed Commons but faced Lords' obstruction. The **Parliament Act of 1911** allowed Commons to eventually override Lords, ensuring Home Rule would become law by 1914. However, the prospect of civil conflict in Ulster—along with the outbreak of World War I—deferred implementation. Thus, the "Irish question" remained unresolved, sowing seeds for the later Irish War of Independence (1919–1921) and the partition of Ireland in the early 1920s.

19.7 Cultural and Scientific Developments

Literature and the Arts
Edwardian Britain produced notable authors who captured the era's shifts:

- **Joseph Conrad**: Explored colonialism and moral ambiguity in *Heart of Darkness* (1899), *Lord Jim* (1900).
- **E.M. Forster**: Critiqued social class and repression in novels like *Howards End* (1910).
- **H.G. Wells**: Used science fiction to comment on social evolution (*The War of the Worlds*, *The Time Machine*).

The theater saw innovations, including **George Bernard Shaw**'s witty dramas lampooning social conventions and **John Galsworthy**'s explorations of class constraints. Meanwhile, art movements like the **Arts and Crafts** tradition continued, though new modernist impulses would soon emerge in painting, sculpture, and design.

Science and Technology
Britain remained at the forefront of technological progress:

1. **Automobiles and Flight**: Early 20th-century improvements in motor vehicles and the first powered flights drew fascination. British engineers tested airships and airplanes, though continental pioneers often led in aeronautics.
2. **Wireless Communication**: Guglielmo Marconi established the first transatlantic wireless signals in 1901, leveraging British funding and infrastructure.
3. **Physics Revolution**: International figures such as Max Planck and Albert Einstein advanced theoretical physics abroad, impacting British scientific circles. In Cambridge, scientists like J.J. Thomson and Ernest Rutherford probed atomic structure, foreshadowing radical shifts in understanding matter.

Social Sciences and Psychology
Scholars engaged more deeply with the concept of society as an object of systematic study. The London School of Economics (founded 1895) expanded research in economics and political science. Psychology began to gain ground, though Freudian ideas had only a limited immediate audience. All these intellectual stirrings contributed to a sense of rapid change, unsettling comfortable Victorian certainties.

19.8 Foreign Affairs and the Road to War

Ententes and Alliances
The early 1900s saw Britain, alarmed by Germany's naval expansion, reorient its foreign policy:

- **Entente Cordiale (1904)** with France ended centuries of rivalry, leading to cooperation.
- **Anglo-Russian Entente (1907)** formed a "Triple Entente" (Britain, France, Russia) to counter the **Triple Alliance** of Germany, Austria-Hungary, and Italy.

Britain attempted to maintain the "balance of power" in Europe, but tension with Germany escalated amid naval arms races and colonial rivalries—particularly in Morocco (1905, 1911 crises). Edward VII's frequent European tours were partly diplomatic efforts to keep allies close.

Naval Arms Race
In 1906, Britain launched the revolutionary battleship **HMS Dreadnought**, outclassing existing vessels. Germany responded with its own dreadnoughts, igniting a race that consumed vast resources. Public opinion fixated on the "naval scare," urging the Admiralty to "build more ships." Although Britain maintained naval superiority, the sense of looming conflict overshadowed domestic politics by the early 1910s.

The July Crisis (1914)
The assassination of Archduke Franz Ferdinand in Sarajevo (June 28, 1914) triggered diplomatic ultimatums across Europe. Britain hesitated—many Liberals opposed war unless absolutely necessary. However, Germany's violation of Belgian neutrality (protected by the 1839 Treaty of London) and the threat to France compelled Britain to declare war on August 4, 1914. The nation entered **World War I** (known then as the Great War) with a mixture of patriotism and apprehension, marking the end of the Edwardian idyll.

19.9 Summary of Chapter 19

Between 1901 and 1914, Britain stood at its imperial apex while confronting transformative social pressures:

- **Monarchical Transition**: Edward VII and George V presided over an empire more interconnected and media-driven, though day-to-day governance increasingly depended on evolving parliamentary democracy.
- **Imperial Power**: The empire was vast, but criticisms of colonial practices grew; the Boer War and various colonial conflicts tarnished the ideal of a benevolent empire.
- **Domestic Reforms**: The Liberal government's welfare measures—pensions, health, and unemployment insurance—laid the groundwork for a more interventionist state. Women's suffrage campaigns gained momentum, though real progress would wait until after WWI.
- **Ireland and Home Rule**: The push for Irish autonomy nearly sparked civil war, highlighting deep divisions within the United Kingdom.
- **Cultural Dynamism**: Literature, art, and science flourished, reflecting both pride in progress and anxieties about change.
- **Diplomatic Rivalries**: A new alignment with France and Russia, plus a naval race with Germany, paved the way to European conflict. When war erupted in 1914, Britain embarked on a cataclysmic struggle that would shatter prewar assumptions about empire, society, and power.

Thus, the Edwardian era ended abruptly with Britain plunging into a war that would define the first half of the 20th century. These years forged the high point of British confidence, as well as the seeds of upheaval that would transform the kingdom in the century ahead.

Chapter 20: The Early 1900s and the Road Ahead (1914–1924)

Introduction
If the Edwardian era (1901–1914) symbolized confidence in Britain's imperial mission and social order, the outbreak of **World War I** in August 1914 shattered any lingering illusions of the old European balance. For Britain, the period from 1914 to the early 1920s was dominated by the war's vast demands—mobilizing millions of soldiers, reorganizing the home front, and weathering economic strains. Though the war officially ended in 1918, its aftermath reverberated: revolutions in Russia, the redrawing of Europe's map, and the reshaping of the British Empire, including Ireland's path toward independence.

This final chapter focuses on the Great War's impact on British politics, society, and empire between 1914 and the mid-1920s. While World War I propels us close to "modern times," we remain within a distinctly historical lens, concluding just before the changes that led fully into the later 20th century. We will examine how the war accelerated suffrage reforms, catalyzed new roles for women, and exposed economic vulnerabilities, leading to a world in which Britain's unquestioned global supremacy began to erode.

20.1 Britain Enters the Great War

Initial Reactions (1914)
Britain declared war on Germany on August 4, 1914, primarily over Germany's violation of Belgian neutrality and the perceived threat to France (with whom Britain had the Entente Cordiale). The conflict was widely supported at first, with many Liberals, Conservatives, and even some Labour figures seeing it as a necessary stand against militarism. Recruiting posters featuring Lord Kitchener's pointing finger ("Your Country Needs You") spurred voluntary enlistment in the first months.

Political Changes
Prime Minister **Herbert Henry Asquith** led a Liberal government but soon faced mounting criticism for inadequate war preparations. By 1915, a **Coalition**

Government brought Conservatives and some Labour figures into the cabinet, attempting national unity. As casualties mounted and the war demanded total mobilization, David Lloyd George (then Minister of Munitions) rose in prominence. In December 1916, Lloyd George replaced Asquith as Prime Minister, heading a smaller War Cabinet and centralizing decision-making.

Military Commitment
The British Expeditionary Force (BEF), initially small compared to continental armies, rapidly expanded. By 1916–1917, conscription was introduced (the Military Service Acts) after voluntary recruitment fell short. Millions served on the Western Front in France and Belgium, enduring trench warfare at battles like the Somme (1916) and Passchendaele (1917). Britain's global empire also provided troops and resources—from Canadians and Australians at Vimy Ridge and Gallipoli to Indian soldiers in Mesopotamia.

20.2 The Home Front and Social Transformation

Economic Mobilization
War demanded an unprecedented coordination of industries:

1. **Munitions**: Under Lloyd George's Ministry of Munitions, factories reorganized or newly built churned out shells, guns, and explosives. Skilled labor shortages led to the employment of women in large numbers.
2. **Shipping and Blockade**: The German U-boat campaign threatened Britain's imports, forcing stricter rationing and better convoy systems. Merchant shipping losses hurt the economy and heightened submarine warfare tension.
3. **Agricultural Reforms**: With the closure of European grain sources, Britain strove to expand domestic production. Measures like the Corn Production Act (1917) guaranteed minimum prices to encourage farmers.

Role of Women
The war accelerated changes in women's labor and social status. In munitions factories, transport, and agricultural "Land Army," women filled roles previously reserved for men. Although many returned to traditional domestic work post-war, the experience broadened horizons. Politically, women's war service bolstered the suffrage cause. Suffragette organizations suspended militant activities to support the war effort. This goodwill, combined with recognition of

women's contributions, paved the way for partial women's enfranchisement in 1918.

Civil Liberties and Propaganda

Wartime legislation, like the Defence of the Realm Act (DORA), curtailed certain freedoms—allowing censorship, restrictions on travel, and control over industrial disputes. Government propaganda used new mass media to maintain morale, demonizing the German foe and valorizing British troops. Despite the official narrative of unity, dissent existed—some socialist pacifists and conscientious objectors faced imprisonment or ostracism. Yet overall, the war demanded collective sacrifice, forging a sense of shared endeavor (and shared grief) across class lines.

20.3 Key Battles and War-Weariness

Western Front Stalemate

From 1914 onward, the Western Front's trench lines stretched from the North Sea to Switzerland, producing a gruesome war of attrition. Britain's major engagements included:

- **Battle of the Somme (July–November 1916)**: Notable for its horrific first day (57,000 British casualties), it epitomized the futility of head-on assaults against entrenched positions.
- **Battle of Passchendaele (July–November 1917)**: Fought amid mud-choked Belgian fields; Allied gains were minimal compared to massive losses.

These battles inflicted staggering casualties and sapped national morale, though propaganda often framed them as necessary to wear down German forces.

Naval Warfare

Britain's Grand Fleet clashed with the German High Seas Fleet at the **Battle of Jutland (1916)**—the war's largest naval engagement. While neither side claimed a decisive victory, Britain's blockade of Germany continued, contributing to German economic hardship. U-boat attacks on merchant shipping threatened Britain's lifeline, leading to rationing at home.

War in the Air

Aviation was in its infancy, but the Royal Flying Corps (later the Royal Air Force, founded in 1918) engaged in reconnaissance, aerial combat, and occasional bombing raids. Germany's zeppelin raids on British towns, though limited in strategic effect, introduced civilians to the reality of aerial bombardment—an ominous harbinger of future warfare.

Public Sentiment
By 1917, war-weariness had grown. Memorial rolls soared, families struggled with loss, and food shortages bit deeper. Russia's exit from the conflict after the Bolshevik Revolution (late 1917) worried Britain, while the entry of the United States in April 1917 offered new hope. Lloyd George juggled appeasing the military top brass and responding to public demands for a resolution.

20.4 The End of the War and the Aftermath

Armistice and Peace Treaties
Germany's final offensive in spring 1918 failed. With Allied support from fresh American troops, the tide turned in the Hundred Days Offensive. Germany sought an armistice, signed on November 11, 1918. Britain emerged as one of the victors, but the human cost was immense: over 700,000 British and Dominion military dead, with millions wounded or traumatized.

At the **Paris Peace Conference (1919)**, Lloyd George joined French Premier Georges Clemenceau and U.S. President Woodrow Wilson to shape the postwar settlement. The **Treaty of Versailles** imposed punitive reparations on Germany and reconfigured European borders. Britain gained mandates over former German and Ottoman territories (e.g., Palestine, Iraq), effectively enlarging the empire. Yet managing these new territories proved costly, and criticism grew over perceived imperial overreach.

Home Front Challenges
Returning servicemen faced a tough economy. The government's promise of a "land fit for heroes" often rang hollow. Strikes proliferated in industries such as coal, transport, and steel, as workers demanded better wages and conditions. Labour's parliamentary strength grew—by 1922, the party was a formidable force, challenging the postwar Conservative-dominated cabinets. The 1919 **Police Strike** in Liverpool and unrest in Glasgow's "Battle of George Square" illustrated the tinderbox atmosphere.

20.5 Political Shifts: The 1918 Reform Act and Rise of Labour

Representation of the People Act (1918)
Even before the war's end, Parliament enacted a sweeping franchise reform:

- **Enfranchised Most Men** over 21 (or 19 for demobilized soldiers), removing older property restrictions.
- **Granted Women Over 30** the vote if they met minimal property qualifications—still not full equality, but a major milestone.
- **Expanded the Electorate** from around 7.7 million voters in 1912 to about 21 million in 1918, making Britain significantly more democratic.

Postwar Elections
The "khaki election" of December 1918 returned Lloyd George as Prime Minister, nominally leading a coalition dominated by Conservatives. This government struggled with postwar reconstruction, soldier demobilization, and economic difficulties. By 1922, internal fissures and public discontent with scandals (like the "Honours Scandal," where peerages were allegedly sold) ended Lloyd George's premiership. The Conservatives took over under Andrew Bonar Law, later Stanley Baldwin, marking a shift toward a more stable right-wing governance—though with Labour waiting in the wings.

Labour's Growth
Under leaders like **Ramsay MacDonald**, Labour capitalized on widespread working-class frustration. The **Miners' Federation**, railway unions, and other trade union blocs provided a base of electoral support. The party's moderate socialist program, focusing on nationalization of key industries and social welfare, attracted voters disillusioned by austerity measures and perceived neglect. By the early 1920s, Labour replaced the Liberal Party as the main alternative to the Conservatives, a tectonic change in British politics.

20.6 Ireland's Turmoil and Partition

Easter Rising (1916)
During the war, Irish republicans staged the **Easter Rising** in Dublin, aiming to secure independence while Britain was preoccupied. The rebellion was suppressed, but the harsh British response—executions of rebel leaders—galvanized nationalist sentiment. Sinn Féin, a republican party, gained popularity, rejecting Westminster altogether.

Anglo-Irish War (1919–1921)

In the postwar period, the newly elected Sinn Féin MPs declared an Irish Republic in 1919, inaugurating guerrilla warfare by the Irish Republican Army (IRA) against British forces. London responded with auxiliary police units, the "Black and Tans," known for brutal reprisals. Violence escalated, with assassinations, reprisals, and civilian casualties mounting.

Partition and the Irish Free State (1921–1922)

Eventually, the **Anglo-Irish Treaty** (December 1921) ended hostilities. Southern Ireland became the **Irish Free State** in 1922, a self-governing Dominion within the British Commonwealth, while six predominantly Protestant counties in Ulster remained part of the United Kingdom as **Northern Ireland**. This partition, though easing the immediate conflict, left a legacy of division and sectarian tension that would persist for decades. The Irish Civil War (1922–1923) further complicated matters. For Britain, losing most of Ireland was a profound moment, showing that the empire could be contested even "at home."

20.7 Society, Culture, and a Changing Empire

Postwar Society

After 1918, British society wrestled with the memory of war. War memorials dotted towns across the land, honoring the fallen. The "lost generation" narrative shaped literature, with authors like **Siegfried Sassoon**, **Wilfred Owen**, and **Robert Graves** capturing the horror of trench warfare. "Shell shock" (later known as PTSD) afflicted thousands of returning veterans, challenging prior assumptions about masculinity and mental health.

Women's Shifting Roles

The partial enfranchisement of women in 1918 (and equal suffrage in 1928, slightly beyond our scope) was but one change. Many middle-class women had tasted financial and personal independence during the war. Though the push for women to return to domestic life was strong in 1920s Britain, the expansion of female employment in offices, retail, and teaching signaled continuing evolution. The loosening of some social norms—evident in fashion (shorter skirts, bobbed hair) and leisure—caused moral panics among conservative commentators.

Imperial Reflection

Britain exited the war physically intact, unlike the devastated landscapes of France and Belgium. Yet the empire's expense—financially and in lives—invited reevaluation. Former Dominions like Canada and Australia, having fought under their own flags, demanded greater autonomy. The **Statute of Westminster (1931)**, which would formalize Dominion legislative independence, loomed ahead. Meanwhile, anti-colonial sentiment simmered in India under Gandhi's leadership, though Britain continued to rely on imperial resources to maintain global status.

20.8 Economic Strains and the End of an Era

Financial Burdens
The war had disrupted global trade, leaving Britain heavily indebted to the United States. Prewar gold reserves were depleted, and Britain's export markets faced new competition from rising industrial nations. The shift from war production to peacetime goods was uneven, leading to strikes and high unemployment in industries like coal. Efforts to return to the **Gold Standard** at prewar parity (1925) under Chancellor Winston Churchill proved controversial, allegedly harming exports.

Fall of Lloyd George and Rise of Baldwin
The coalition that had sustained Lloyd George frayed under economic crises and perceived corruption. In 1922, Conservatives at the **Carlton Club meeting** withdrew support for the coalition, forcing Lloyd George's resignation. Andrew Bonar Law briefly took over, followed by Stanley Baldwin, who shaped interwar Conservative governance with a focus on compromise and moral leadership. Baldwin's paternalistic approach emphasized national unity, though unrest in mining and heavy industry would soon boil over (e.g., the General Strike of 1926, slightly outside our timeframe).

Cultural Aftershocks
The war's psychic legacy resonated in literature and the arts. Modernist writers—**T.S. Eliot**, **Virginia Woolf**, **James Joyce** (though Irish, published in Britain)—challenged linear storytelling, reflecting the fragmentation of old certainties. Fashions changed (the "flapper" style in women's dress, simpler men's suits), amusements like cinema expanded, and radios began to appear in middle-class homes. The traumatic experience of war shaped a generation's worldview, dampening the imperial triumphalism that had characterized the pre-1914 era.

20.9 Conclusion: Britain on the Threshold of Modern Times

By the mid-1920s, the United Kingdom had endured four grueling years of total war, lost a significant portion of Ireland, and witnessed fundamental shifts in its political and social fabric. The empire remained vast, but the conflict had revealed vulnerabilities. Politically, the electorate was far broader than ever, and a new party—Labour—was on track to challenge Conservative rule. Women were partially enfranchised and increasingly visible in public life, while the aristocratic grip on power waned further. Industrial relations were contentious, with looming strike action. Meanwhile, Britain's global financial dominance faced strong competition, indicating the erosion of absolute economic supremacy it had enjoyed in the Victorian era.

Though we stop short of truly "modern times," the era from 1914 to the early 1920s illuminates how Britain pivoted away from the old structures of empire and aristocracy to a more democratic, if uncertain, polity. The Great War shattered illusions, forging new national narratives of sacrifice and heroism, but also planting seeds of discontent and radicalism. Over the next decades, these forces would reshape the United Kingdom in ways unimaginable at the dawn of the 20th century.

20.10 Summary of Chapter 20

From 1914 to the early 1920s, Britain faced an all-consuming conflict that remade its politics, society, and empire:

1. **World War I**: Britain's entry into a total war required massive mobilization, leading to conscription, an expanded industrial output, and widespread social controls. The trenches on the Western Front epitomized the war's brutal stalemate, with major battles like the Somme inflicting catastrophic losses.
2. **Coalition Politics and Home Front**: War unity brought together Liberals, Conservatives, and some Labour figures, eventually placing Lloyd George as Prime Minister (1916). Women entered factories in unprecedented numbers, and rationing along with government propaganda shaped daily life.
3. **Costly Victory**: The 1918 armistice left Britain victorious but drained. The peace settlement at Versailles restructured Europe, awarding Britain new

mandates but raising ethical and financial concerns. Postwar demobilization and unemployment fueled strikes and social unrest.
4. **Franchise Expansion**: The Representation of the People Act (1918) enfranchised most adult men and some women, vastly increasing the electorate. This, coupled with Labour's rise, spelled the decline of the Liberal Party and the transformation of British party politics.
5. **Ireland's Partition**: The Easter Rising and Anglo-Irish War led to the partition of Ireland in 1922, with Northern Ireland remaining in the UK and the Irish Free State emerging as a Dominion, a profound shift that ended centuries of direct British rule over most of the island.
6. **Cultural and Economic Shifts**: War memorials, modernist literature, and public mourning defined the immediate postwar culture. Economically, Britain struggled with debts and lost markets, and the empire's future seemed less assured.

By 1924, the nation found itself in a new age. Though still not fully modern in the sense of the mid-to-late 20th century, Britain had moved far from the Victorian world. Democracy broadened, Ireland largely departed, and war-weary citizens looked for stability. The shadows of future challenges—economic turbulence, the rise of new ideologies, and looming international conflicts—stretched ahead, but those lie beyond our historical scope here. Thus, we conclude our account of the United Kingdom's history before fully entering modern times, having traced its arc from prehistoric settlement to an empire tested by the crucible of World War I and evolving toward a more democratic, if still complex, society.

Help Us Share Your Thoughts!

Dear reader,

Thank you for spending your time with this book. We hope it brought you enjoyment and a few new ideas to think about. If there was anything that didn't work for you, or if you have suggestions on how we can improve, please let us know at **kontakt@skriuwer.com**. Your feedback means a lot to us and helps us make our books even better.

If you enjoyed this book, we would be very grateful if you left a review on the site where you purchased it. Your review not only helps other readers find our books, but also encourages us to keep creating more stories and materials that you'll love.

By choosing Skriuwer, you're also supporting **Frisian**—a minority language mainly spoken in the northern Netherlands. Although **Frisian** has a rich history, the number of speakers is shrinking, and it's at risk of dying out. Your purchase helps fund resources to preserve and promote this language, such as educational programs and learning tools. If you'd like to learn more about Frisian or even start learning it yourself, please visit **www.learnfrisian.com**.

Thank you for being part of our community. We look forward to sharing more books with you in the future.

Warm regards,
The Skriuwer Team